# Softball Secrets!

## Solving the Mysteries of the Mental Game

DR. CURT ICKES

Copyright © 2024 by Dr. Curt Ickes
First Paperback Edition: 2024

All rights reserved. No part of this book may be used or reproduced in any form or by any electronic or mechanical means including information storage and retrieval systems — except in the case of brief quotations embodied in critical articles or reviews, without written permission from its author and from its publisher. Printed in the United States.

IRC Holdings Ltd
Ashland, OH 44805

ISBN: 9798343311952
Published by KDP

Edited by: Cynthia Hilston, Olivia Fisher
Cover Illustration by: Hedri on Fiverr

# Softball Secrets!

## Solving the Mysteries of the Mental Game

**Parents and coaches, welcome to a game-changer!**

Are you ready to help your young softball players unlock their full potential? *Softball Secrets!* is packed with essential mental game skills for players ages 10-14, skills that go beyond the field and into everyday life. This book teaches young athletes how to handle pressure, recover from mistakes, manage their emotions, and build unshakable confidence. These lessons aren't just for sports; they help shape resilient, confident young people.

**Parents:** Imagine watching your child step onto the field with confidence, knowing they have the tools to face any challenge, both in softball and in life. The story of Ava, Zoe, Addie, Sophia, and the Southport Sting will inspire your young athlete as they see relatable struggles and triumphs. Through engaging storytelling, this book makes complex concepts simple and fun to learn. And with quick review activities at the end of each chapter, your child can solidify what they've learned while staying excited about the game!

**Coaches:** This book isn't just for individual players—it's specifically designed for teams. The included coaches' guide is your playbook for turning these lessons into powerful team practices. Imagine your team not only improving their game skills but also speaking the same "mental game language," supporting each other, and growing stronger as a unit. By studying *Softball Secrets!* together, chapter by chapter, you'll be building the foundation for success. Your team will crush it on and off the field with this book, so go all in and get it for everyone.

**Congratulations on taking the next step!** You're giving your players an invaluable advantage—the gift of mental toughness and resilience. With *Softball Secrets!*, you'll see them grow not only as players but as individuals, making the game of softball more fulfilling and fun for everyone.

Dr. Curt Ickes

### *Sport Psychology Books by Dr. Curt Ickes*

These bestselling books are all available on Amazon!

### Baseball Books
*Win the Next Pitch! (Ages 8-12)*
*Pitch by Pitch! (Ages 10-14)*
*Mental Toughness: Getting the Edge (Ages 15 and older)*

### Softball Books
*You Got This! (Ages 8-12)*
*You Got This! 2 (Ages 8-12)*
*Softball Secrets! (Ages 10-14)*

# Table of Contents

Chapter 1 – A Box Full of Softball Secrets ......................................... 1

Chapter 2 – Just Win the Next Pitch! ............................................... 15

Chapter 3 – Be a Leader: Control Your Energy and Attitude ....... 25

Chapter 4 – Reset and Win: Secrets to Staying Cool ..................... 35

Chapter 5 – These Bulldogs Bite! ..................................................... 47

Chapter 6 – Focus Your Flashlight: Blocking Out Distractions ..... 59

Chapter 7 – Talk Like a Champ: Make Your Mind Your MVP ........ 69

Chapter 8 – Stop Thinking So You Can Start Hitting! .................. 79

Chapter 9 – The Secret Skill: Seeing It Before You Do It ............ 89

Chapter 10 – No More Doubt: How to Play with Confidence ..... 97

Chapter 11 – Southport's City Championship: Time for the Sting to Shine 105

Chapter 12 – Katie, Is That You? ................................................... 119

Coaches' Guide ................................................................................. 135

Concentration Grids ......................................................................... 148

Acknowledgments ............................................................................ 151

About the Author ............................................................................. 153

# CHAPTER 1

# A Box Full of Softball Secrets

The afternoon sun peeked through tall oak trees casting a golden glow on the sidewalks of Southport. Four girls walked home from the Southport Sting's softball practice, laughing and chatting. Ava, a tall blond girl with a confident stride, led the way, her eyes scanning the street for anything interesting. As the team's star hitter, she was a natural leader.

Zoe, with reddish hair bouncing like a flame, walked beside Ava. The Sting's shortstop fanned her face, trying to cool off after a tough practice. Behind them, Sophia, the team's pitcher, winced while inspecting a long scrape on her arm. Addie, known as Tech Girl, trailed behind, her eyes glued to her phone as if the rest of the world didn't exist.

"I can't believe you almost hit the fence today, Addie!" Ava spun around with a wide grin. "That was awesome. You crushed it!"

Addie glanced up from her phone, her cheeks turning pink. "Thanks," she said with a shy smile. "I just wish I could do that in a real game. I get so nervous. At practice, I'm fine, but when it counts…" She fiddled with the phone, her voice trailing off.

"Same here," Zoe added, her eyes dropping to the ground. "For me, it's when I make an error. If I miss a ball or make a bad throw, I freeze the next time a grounder comes my way."

"Yeah, and my confidence disappears as soon as I walk a batter," Sophia added, frowning. "We've got to figure it out before the city tournament next month."

Ava was about to reply when something caught her eye. "Whoa, check that out!" she blurted, pointing to a large yard sale sign in front of a big old rundown house. The house, with peeling paint and an overgrown lawn, seemed to hide a thousand secrets.

"Looks like someone bought the place and is fixing it up," Zoe said, craning her neck. "It's been empty for years."

"I always thought it was spooky, maybe even haunted," Addie whispered, wrapping a strand of hair around her finger.

"Let's go see!" Zoe's eyes sparkled with excitement.

Addie paused, her eyes scanning the broken-down house. "I don't know about this…"

"Oh, come on. Let's just look," Ava said, waving the group forward.

The girls walked up the cracked driveway, their sneakers crunching over weeds. The house loomed over them, its dark, empty windows watching like eyes. The yard was cluttered with old furniture, pictures, and tables stacked with boxes.

Ava's eyes landed on a big box tucked under a table. She kneeled, drawn to the glint of trophies poking out of the top.

"Wow, look at this!" Ava's eyes widened. "They're softball trophies, and they look super old."

Slowly opening one of the crumpled flaps, she peeked inside. "Everything in here is all about softball!"

A woman stepped out from behind a table, wiping her hands with a rag. "Hi! I'm Debbie Smith, the new owner," she said with a friendly smile. "I found that box in the attic. No clue who it belonged to. The house has been empty for years."

The girls exchanged eager glances.

"How much for the box?" Ava asked, her excitement bubbling over.

Debbie's smile widened. "You girls seem to love softball. Take it—it's free!"

Ava's eyes were saucers. "Wow, really?"

Debbie's eyes crinkled with amusement. "Yes, really. You girls will be doing me a favor by taking it. Goodness knows I've got plenty to clean out."

Ava exchanged an eager look with her friends.

"Thank you!" they shouted together.

As Ava lifted the box, a soft whisper floated past her ear, like someone saying her name. She froze, her heart pounding. "Did you hear that?" she asked.

"Hear what?" Sophia asked, furrowing her brow.

"I thought I heard…" Ava's voice trailed off. "Never mind."

Zoe laughed. "You're hearing things, Ava. Maybe you need to rest up when you get home."

Addie and Sophia shook their heads.

Ava shrugged and tugged the heavy box toward herself. Walking down the driveway, her arms burned from the weight, but she didn't mind. "Let's take this to my treehouse and see what's inside," Ava suggested.

"Great idea!" Zoe replied. "I'll text my mom that I'm headed to your place."

Addie and Sophia grabbed their phones. "We'll do the same," they chimed, their thumbs tapping away.

"I can carry it for a bit," Addie said, reaching out her arms. Her usual shyness disappeared in the excitement of the moment.

"Are you sure? It's pretty heavy," Ava asked, both worried and grateful.

"Yeah, I got it!" Addie said, slipping her arms under the box with determination.

With every step, the girls' excitement grew. Soon they reached Ava's cozy two-story house with its big backyard. They wasted no time and headed straight for the treehouse.

Perched high in a giant oak, Ava's treehouse was their secret hangout. It was where they'd planned sleepovers, dreamed of winning games, and now, where they'd solve a mystery. The girls scrambled up the ladder, nearly tripping over each other in their rush.

"Hurry up, Sophia!" Zoe shouted from above.

"I'm coming!" Sophia giggled, pulling herself up the ladder as the last in line.

Ava set the box in the middle, and the girls sat cross-legged around it, their faces lighting up with anticipation. Sunlight filtered through the treehouse windows, casting warm rays over the friends. The smell of pine boards and the sounds of rustling leaves surrounded them.

Ava unpacked the box quickly, handing trophies to Sophia and a worn glove to Zoe.

"These trophies are ancient," Sophia said, running her fingers over the faded lettering.

"Look at this glove!" Zoe said, as she inspected it. "It's worn out. Whoever owned it used it a ton."

"Is there a name on it?" Ava asked, leaning in.

"Nope. Just some faded initials—maybe K.P., but it's hard to tell," Zoe replied, handing the glove to Ava.

"It could be K.P. or maybe K.F.," Ava said. "We've got to figure out who owned this box. Sophia, are there any names on the trophies?"

Sophia turned them over carefully, one by one. "They're all from the 1980s. They just say, 'First Place' or 'Tournament Champions.' No names, no city, no tournament name—nothing." Her face scrunched.

Sophia kept studying the trophies, gently setting each one against the wall. Every trophy seemed to carry a story, but without names, those stories stayed hidden.

Ava pulled out a handful of medals. "Check these out, Addie."

Addie examined the dull medals and then passed them to Zoe. "There aren't any names on them, just 'Champions' and 'MVP.' Whoever she was, she must've been really good."

Zoe nodded, still scanning the medals. "If only we knew which tournaments these were from. We need more clues."

The girls exchanged puzzled looks.

"I know, but all we've got to go on so far are the initials on that old glove," Ava said. "That's not much, but maybe we'll find more clues."

Ava reached into the box again and pulled out an old softball. "Look at this!" She squinted and read the faded inscription. "'First Over-The-Fence Home Run. May 14, 1983. Southport 6, Wilmington 5.'"

Addie's eyes brightened. "That's another clue! She must've played for one of those teams."

Ava nodded. "Addie, you're in charge of keeping track of all the clues, okay?"

Zoe nudged Addie with a playful grin. "With Tech Girl on the case, we'll crack this mystery for sure!"

"On it! I'll save the clues on my phone and send them to everyone. So far, we know she was a great player in the 1980s. Her initials might be K.P. or K.F., and she played for either Southport or Wilmington." Addie grinned, her thumbs moving quickly.

Ava dug her hands deep into the box. "Whoa, this might be the best find yet," she whispered. She carefully lifted a thick, dusty journal from the box.

The girls leaned in, their eyes wide with curiosity.

The cover was plain, with a title written in neat handwriting. Together, they read it aloud.

"*Softball Secrets.*"

Ava slowly opened the journal. The headline on the page read, "Use the Secrets in This Journal to Play Your Best Softball."

"This is what our team needs," Zoe said enthusiastically.

Ava nodded, still staring at the page. "We're good, but we can always get better."

"Maybe there's something in here to help me stay calm during games," Addie whispered.

"Yeah, maybe there's a way to stop getting mad when I mess up," Sophia added.

Ava squinted at the page. "Hey, check this out. Someone wrote a bunch of letters."

Sgd rdbqds sn rnesazkk: Itrs vhm sgd mdws ohsbg!

The girls moved closer, sounding out the letters together.

"It looks like a secret code, but what could it mean?" Sophia bit her lower lip. "There are doodles, too. Do you think they mean anything?"

"It's definitely a code. I'm not sure about the doodles, though. Everyone take a picture, and let's try to figure this out tonight," Addie said.

# Use the Secrets in This Journal to Play Your Best Softball.

Sgd rdbqds an rnesazkk itrs vbm sgd mdws ohsbg!

I  Softball!

SMS

Ava turned another page, and something small and crinkly slid out, floating to the floor. The girls jumped and then crowded closer, their eyes wide with curiosity.

"What is it?" Zoe whispered.

Ava bent down and carefully picked it up. The paper was neatly folded, the edges yellowed and torn, like it had been hidden for years.

The girls exchanged grins. "Open it!" Sophia urged.

Ava carefully unfolded the paper. It was a letter, faded and hard to read.

Hi there!

I started playing softball when I was young, and over time, I learned some mental game secrets that helped me play my best. I figured out how to stay calm, how to remain focused, and how to shake off mistakes so that I was always ready for the very next pitch in a game. The skills in this journal made a huge difference in my games, so I wrote them down.

Someday, when I grow up, I want to make this into a real book for girls who love softball. But for now, I'm leaving these tips here in case someone finds them and needs help on the field. I hope these skills help you like they helped me.

Good luck, and remember—always be ready for the next pitch!

—Katie

"Her name is Katie! The K stands for Katie! Another clue!" Addie gasped, her fingers tapping quickly on her phone as she added it to the growing list of clues.

The girls nodded as Ava gingerly tucked the letter into the journal. They couldn't wait to discover what other secrets Katie had left behind.

Zoe's eyes widened. "Let's see what else is in here."

Ava slowly flipped through the journal, its yellowed pages filled with typed notes and little sketches of players in action. The pages were divided into sections: "Energy & Attitude," "Control Your Emotions & Resetting," "Dealing with Distractions," "Positive Self-Talk," "Pre-Pitch Routines," "Visualization," and "Confidence."

"This is amazing. There's so much stuff in here," Ava whispered, her eyes shining. "We all want to get better at softball, and this is our chance. We've got to read it together."

Addie, still staring at the journal as if it held all the answers in the world, whispered, "This could change everything for us."

"What if this book helps us win the city tournament?" Sophia wondered aloud.

Zoe's eyes sparkled. "This could be our secret weapon!"

Just then, Sophia's phone buzzed. She glanced at it and sighed. "Mom says it's time for dinner. I gotta go."

"Me, too," Addie said, her thumbs crawling as she reluctantly sent a text to her mom.

As Ava gently closed the book, a shadow flickered past the treehouse window. Her heart skipped a beat. "Did you see that?" she whispered. A shiver ran up her spine, despite the warm, humid air.

"See what?" Zoe asked, following Ava's gaze.

Ava stared at the window a moment longer, then turned toward her friends. She laughed it off. "Um, nothing. Must've just been a shadow from a branch or something."

"Or maybe our star hitter really does need a nap," Sophia joked.

The shadow was long gone.

Ava waved her off. "Anyway, we've got this neat treasure to focus on." She cradled the journal as if it were a fragile, precious treasure. "Let's meet here tomorrow before practice to dig into this mystery. How's one o'clock?"

"Sounds good," Zoe said, excitement bubbling beneath her forced patience.

"Sure!" Addie nodded.

"I'll be here! We'll learn these secrets and maybe even solve the mystery of who Katie was," Sophia said.

The girls nodded eagerly, their imaginations buzzing with the thrill of the unknown. They scrambled down the ladder, their feet thudding softly as they hit the ground. As they walked home, the sun dipped lower, casting long shadows across the sidewalk.

The old box, filled with forgotten treasures, had sparked something special in them. It wasn't just about trophies and medals—it was about connecting with someone who loved the game as much as they did. Their minds buzzed with thoughts of the secrets still hidden in that old journal.

**Solve These Mystery Questions!**

1. The girls found a journal with softball secrets. If you found it, what would you want to learn?

2. Addie was nervous about performing well in a real game. Have you ever felt nervous before a game or test? How did you handle those feelings?

3. Can you figure out the secret code? What do you think the doodles on that page mean?

CHAPTER 2

# Just Win the Next Pitch!

The next afternoon, the girls climbed back into Ava's treehouse, their hearts pounding as they circled around the dusty old journal.

Addie's eyes lit up. "Did anyone crack the code?"

The rest of the girls shared blank looks.

Then Ava said, "No, but I'm guessing you did, Tech Girl, with that brilliant mind of yours."

"I sure did! You swap each letter with the one that comes next in the alphabet."

Ava's jaw dropped. "See? I knew you were brilliant."

Addie blushed. "It wasn't that hard."

"Well, I never would've thought of that. What does it say?" Ava asked, eyes shining.

Addie unfolded a piece of paper, her hands shaking as she held it up. Underneath the code, Addie had written the answer.

*Just Win the Next Pitch!*

**S g d   r d b q d s   s n   r n e s a z k k:   I t r s   v h m   s g d   m d w   s   o h s b g!**

**The secret to softball: Just win the next pitch!**

Sophia grinned and bumped fists with Addie. "Nice work, Tech Girl! Do the doodles mean anything?"

Addie squinted as she rubbed her chin, then pointed to the page.

"There's a diamond and a girl here. *Diamond girl.* Do you think that could've been Katie's nickname?"

"That totally makes sense!" Zoe's eyes brightened. "We'll keep trying to figure out the rest of these as we go."

"Let's find out what else is inside." Ava carefully opened the journal, her fingers brushing its worn edges.

"Look at this title," she said, pointing to the first line on the page.

## *The Main Goal in Every Game is to Be 100% Ready to Win the Next Pitch*

Ava kept reading. "In softball, the main goal is to be ready to play your best on the next pitch. Don't worry about the whole game. Whether you're pitching, hitting, or fielding, **your mind is only on this next pitch.**"

Ava paused and looked up.

The girls leaned in closer, hanging on every word.

"Why is this so important? Because every pitch is a chance to change the game. It could be the one that gets you out of trouble or drives in the winning run. If you're distracted by past plays or your own thoughts, you'll miss that chance. Great players know it's all about doing everything they can to be 100% ready for the next pitch. Win the pitch, and you win at-bat. Win at-bats, and your team wins innings. Win innings, and you win games."

"That makes sense. If I'm mad about swinging at a bad pitch, the next one zooms by before I know it," Addie said. "It's like my brain is so cluttered I can't react."

"When I stay stuck on a wild pitch or a walk, the bad pitches just keep coming," Sophia added.

Ava nodded and read on. "Softball is easier when you take it one pitch at a time."

"I try, but it's hard!" Sophia said. "When I can't throw strikes, I freak out. I worry we're going to lose, and my mind races. It makes pitching a lot tougher."

"Yeah, and when I get two strikes, I get super nervous. I shake a little, and it feels like everyone's watching and waiting for me to strike out," Addie added.

Ava turned to Zoe. "What about you?"

"I'm the same way," Zoe said with a sigh. "After a mistake, I still think about it instead of the next pitch that's coming. I doubt myself, and then I end up missing the next grounder."

"So, the trick is to focus on just winning the very next pitch," Addie said, tapping her tablet.

"But how do we actually do that?" Sophia asked, crossing her arms. "Seems easier said than done."

Ava flipped the page, her eyebrows rising. "Aha! Check out this picture."

"Wow, so this is it! These seven secrets show us how to win the next pitch," Sophia said, eyes wide.

_Softball Secrets!_

The girls leaned in, their eyes glued to the book as Ava's voice filled the treehouse.

**The Seven Secrets: How to Be Ready to Win Every Pitch.**

"Winning the next pitch doesn't happen by accident—you practice it, just like hitting or fielding. These seven skills will help you stay locked in on the next pitch, no matter what happens in a game. I'll teach you all these skills in my journal."

Ava turned the book toward the girls, and they all read silently, soaking up each word.

1. **Play with Energy & an Arrows-Out Attitude:** Great players bring energy to every single pitch. Whether you're cheering in the

dugout or playing on the field, high energy pumps up your team and keeps you sharp. It shows your teammates you're ready and excited to play.

**Always Play with an Arrows-Out Attitude.** This means focusing all your energy on the game, not on yourself or your feelings. Instead of pouting when something goes wrong, attack the next pitch with everything you've got. Don't quit. An 'Arrows-In' attitude is when you feel sorry for yourself. It looks bad to everyone watching, and it doesn't help your team!

Sophia broke the silence. "I didn't play Arrows-Out last game. After they scored three runs in the first inning, I dragged my feet back to the circle, feeling totally defeated. I was definitely Arrows-In."

"I've done that, too, lost energy and started moping. I really need to stop doing that," Zoe said, scrunching her eyebrows.

"Let's see what's next." Ava flipped the page.

2. **Control Your Emotions & Reset After Mistakes:**
    Softball has a lot of ups and downs. You'll feel nervous, frustrated, or even a little scared. Learning how to stay calm, no matter what's happening, helps you play your best.

    **Resetting After a Mistake**
    Mistakes happen. You might strike out or miss a grounder. It's easy to feel bad, but that won't help. Great players don't get stuck on their mistakes. They quickly reset by using the 3 Ts to put the mistake behind them and focus on the next pitch.

3. **Dealing with Distractions:**
   Lots of things can distract you from focusing on the next pitch like the fans, the other team, umpires, or even your own racing thoughts. But you can learn to ignore distractions and just focus on the ball.

Addie typed quickly on her tablet. "She really has some good ideas. I need this one. When I'm up to bat, I always get distracted by my own thoughts."

4. **Use Positive Self-Talk:**
   What you say to yourself matters. If you tell yourself you're a terrible player, it makes the next pitch much harder. Instead, say positive things such as 'I've got this' or 'Let's go!' Positive self-talk keeps you confident and ready for anything.

Zoe nudged Ava with a grin. "You're always the one shouting, 'You got this!' from the dugout."

Ava laughed. "Now you know why I say it—it actually works!"

5. **Use Good Pre-Pitch Routines:**
   A pre-pitch routine is what you do before every pitch to get ready. Most players rely on superstitions, but I'll show you a better way. A routine where every step is important to helping you relax and totally lock in on the next pitch.

6. **Practice Visualization:**
   Visualization is like watching a movie in your mind, but you're the star! Picture yourself hitting a double or fielding a tricky grounder. Visualization gets you ready for big game moments before they happen, so when it's your turn, you're prepared!

Ava grinned, still reading, then looked up from the journal. "I've heard something about this before. I'm definitely going to try it."

7. **Learn to Stay Confident:**
   Every player struggles with confidence sometimes. You'll learn tips and tricks to stay confident and believe in yourself, even when things don't go right.

**Putting It All Together**

To be 100% ready for the next pitch, you've got to put these skills into action. It's going to take time to get good at each one, and that's totally okay. Keep practicing, and before you know it, you'll be ready for whatever the game throws at you. The best players aren't just physically tough—they're mentally tough, too.

"I never thought about it like that," Zoe said. "I knew the mental game was important, but I didn't think you could actually practice it. I thought you either had it, or you didn't."

"Most young players feel the same way because no one teaches them the mental side of the game. But this journal is going to change that for us!" Ava said. "So, what have we learned so far, Addie?"

Addie tapped a few more notes into her tablet, then looked up and read aloud.

1. Every pitch matters. But the most important one is always the next pitch. Our job is to be 100% ready for it. We can't let emotions, the crowd, or past mistakes distract us.

2. This journal will teach us the seven mental game secrets we need to win the next pitch.

3. If we practice these skills, we'll start playing better right away.

"I always thought softball was just about running fast and hitting hard," Sophia said, eyes wide. "But this… changes everything."

Ava nodded, her eyes shining. "If we learn the mental game, we'll be unbeatable."

"You know, I still wonder how we stumbled across this amazing find," Addie added, rubbing her chin, eyes narrowed.

"Maybe you're just thinking too much with that big brain of yours," Zoe teased.

Addie shrugged. "Maybe." Then she looked at Ava. "But didn't you say yesterday that you heard and saw something?"

"Yeah, and the rest of us didn't," Sophia added.

All eyes were on Ava. Her face warmed from the attention. She thought back to those strange passing moments, then shook her head. "It was nothing. Remember how you said I just needed a good night's sleep? Well, I slept like a rock, and I haven't heard or seen anything odd today, have I?"

The girls exchanged looks, then nodded.

Yet, as she stared out the window, Ava couldn't help but wonder what this mystery meant…if anything.

## Solve These Mystery Questions!

1. The code says, "Just win the next pitch." Why is this so important in the game of softball? Can you think of a time when this might have helped you?

2. Katie shared seven skills that help players stay ready for the next pitch. Which one or two skills do you think will help you the most in your next game and why?

CHAPTER 3

# Be a Leader: Control Your Energy and Attitude

After shaking off her thoughts, Ava refocused on the task at hand. "Are we ready to learn the first secrets to winning the next pitch?" she asked, gripping the book tightly.

"Yeah!" the girls shouted together, their voices echoing around the treehouse walls. The girls crowded around, eager for Ava to read. The room grew quiet as she began.

"Control what you can control—your attitude and energy. To be fully ready for the next pitch, take charge of both. You choose whether you have a winning or losing attitude and how much energy you bring to every pitch."

**Attitude is Everything**

The right attitude can turn a good player into a great player. It's easy to feel positive when things go well, but the real test is how you act when things get tough. The best players keep their heads up, stay focused, and never stop trying, no matter what.

There are two types of attitudes: Arrows-In and Arrows-Out.

*What is an Arrows-In attitude?*

An Arrows-In attitude shows up when you start feeling down during a game. Maybe you struck out or made an error, and suddenly, you're thinking, 'Why even try?' You start moping or giving up, letting all your energy turn inward and focusing on feeling bad instead of winning the next pitch.

*What is an Arrows-Out attitude?*

An Arrows-Out attitude is the opposite. With this winning attitude, all your energy points to the game, not to your feelings. Even if things go wrong, you stay focused, positive, and more determined.

Players with an Arrows-Out attitude are tougher to beat. They hustle, cheer for their teammates, and never give up. When you play this way, your teammates, coaches, fans, and even the other team notice.

## You're in Charge of Your Attitude

Here's a secret: You control your attitude! You decide how to react when things don't go right. Will you stay in an Arrows-In mindset or flip the switch to Arrows-Out? Every time you step on the field, the choice is yours.

## How to Play Arrows-Out

1. **Notice How You Feel:** Did you make a mistake? Feeling down? The first step is catching yourself slipping into an Arrows-In attitude. It's normal at first, but the key is to catch it early.

2. **Flip the Switch:** Once you notice it, imagine flipping a switch in your mind. Take a deep breath, decide to quit pouting, and point your energy arrows out toward the game.

3. **Play Hard on Every Pitch:** Remember, every pitch is a fresh start. Coaches, teammates, fans, and your opponents will notice your Arrows-Out attitude. They'll respect your grit and determination. No one appreciates a player who mopes!

4. **Arrows-Out Attitudes Are Contagious:** When you and your teammates play with an Arrows-Out attitude, it spreads like wildfire! Your team will be tougher and keep fighting, no matter the score. Attack each pitch with all you've got, and your team will too! This is how you stage big comebacks.

5. **Play Each Pitch Like It's the First Pitch of the Game:** Think about how you feel at the start of a game—pumped up, full of energy, and focused. That's the Arrows-Out attitude! Practice playing each pitch with that "first pitch of the game" feeling.

Ava paused and looked at each girl. "So, next time you're on the field, remember: You control your attitude. Will you let a mistake drag you down, or will you flip the switch and play with an Arrows-Out attitude? The choice is yours, and it can change how you play—and how much fun you have!"

Sophia nodded. "Wow, I didn't know we could control our attitude like that. I always thought we were just stuck feeling down when things went wrong."

"Yeah, I love how switching from Arrows-In to Arrows-Out spreads through the whole team," Addie added. "It's like a wave!"

"We've had games where we were both Arrows-In and Arrows-Out," Zoe said. "Remember when we played the Bandits in that championship game? We were down early, and nothing was going right, but we didn't mope. We flipped the switch and played Arrows-Out!"

"Yeah! And we came back to beat them!" Addie added.

Ava closed the journal and looked at each of the girls. "When we play Arrows-Out, everyone notices. It shows who we are as a team. The fans, coaches, and the other team respect our fighting spirit. So let's make Arrows-Out the only way the Sting plays!"

Ava flipped the page and read more. "Okay, the next thing you control is your energy level. It's a big one! You know how coaches are always shouting, 'Pick up the energy'? That's because high energy gets you and your team ready for every pitch."

Ava stopped and held the book up. "Check this out. It's an energy meter."

One end was marked "Low" in red, the middle "Medium" in yellow, and the other end "High" in green. A big arrow rested right in the middle.

"This meter tracks a team's energy during a game," Ava said, her voice full of enthusiasm.

She pointed to the arrow, her finger tracing its path. "It moves based on how we act. Remember our last game when we were losing—where was our energy?"

The girls glanced down.

"Low," Sophia muttered.

Zoe nodded. "Yeah, we were way in the red. But why did our energy drop so low?"

Sophia sighed. "Before we even started, my energy was low. I thought we'd lose because that team was so good. I moped around, and it hurt our team's energy more than I realized."

"Also, we were too hard on each other," Addie said, tugging at her hair. "Telling Sophia to pitch better only made it worse, and our energy tanked."

Zoe frowned and shook her head. "After I struck out in the first inning, I didn't hustle out to the field. My energy was low, and that hurt the team."

"Great examples!" Ava said, smiling. "All those things pushed our energy meter into the red. Bad energy spreads fast, but good energy spreads even faster! Katie's journal lists three ways to boost energy during a game. Let's see what they are."

1. **Cheering for Each Other:** Celebrate when a teammate gets a hit or makes a great catch! Simple cheers like "Great job!" or "Way to go!" lift everyone's spirits. When we root for each other, we show we're all in this together, pushing our energy meter toward green.

Ava grinned. "I love it when you guys give me a high five or fist bump after a good hit."

The others nodded, smiling back.

"I get even more fired up when I strike someone out and you all cheer," Sophia added. "I feel my energy soar."

2. **Supporting Each Other After Mistakes:** Mistakes happen in every game. Strong teams don't let one mistake bring down their energy. Instead, they pick each other up. Show your teammates you've got their back.

3. **Body Language Matters:** The way you stand on the field shows everyone—your teammates, the fans, and the other team—how you're feeling. No matter what happens, stand tall with your head up. It tells everyone, "We're still in this!" Bad body language doesn't just bring you down—it brings the whole team's energy down.

Ava added, "Bad body language gives the other team a boost. When their pitcher sees you moping after a strikeout, she can't wait to pitch to you again. It's like telling them, 'We give up.' That's when the energy meter really slides into the red."

Ava closed the journal. "Play with high energy on every pitch. Ask yourself, 'Am I boosting or dragging down our team's energy?' So, are we ready to keep our energy meter in the green all game?"

"Yes!" the girls shouted together.

Addie pointed to the journal. "I've got an idea! Let's make our own energy meter and bring it to practice today!"

Ava's eyes brightened. "Great idea! Let's do it!" She dashed inside and returned with supplies.

Markers squeaked, and paper scraps piled up as the girls quickly got to work on their project. Addie read the notes from her tablet aloud.

1. Attitude and energy are two things every player can control. You're in charge of both.

2. Choose to play with an Arrows-Out attitude—a winning attitude.

3. Instead of feeling sorry for yourself when things go wrong, keep pushing forward and play even harder.

4. Play with high energy on every pitch, every game!

5. Each player controls their own energy.

6. High energy is contagious. When everyone brings it, the whole team plays better.

7. Cheer for each other, support each other after mistakes, and use strong body language to keep our energy in the green.

8. We'll use the energy meter in the dugout to remind us to stay pumped!

When they finished, Ava held the Sting's energy meter high above her head, her smile stretching wide.

"Awesome!" The girls giggled, clapping as Ava slid the arrow into the green zone.

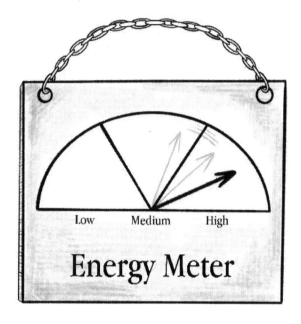

"Coach Moore can hang it in the dugout and move the arrow during games," Ava said, passing it around.

Sophia jumped up, her arm raised above her head, a finger pointed to the sky. "From now on, the Sting will always play Arrows-Out and with high energy!" she declared.

Her teammates stood up and cheered. "Let's go, Sting!"

They climbed down from the treehouse, knowing their journey with Katie's mental game secrets was just beginning. They couldn't wait to see where it would take them next.

**Solve These Mystery Questions!**

1. What are two things all players can control no matter what happens in the game?

2. What does Arrows-Out mean? How is it different from Arrows-In? What happens when players let an Arrows-In attitude take over? How does it affect the team?

3. What can you do if you notice your energy meter slipping into the red during a game?

# CHAPTER 4

# Reset and Win: Secrets to Staying Cool

The next morning, Ava, Zoe, Addie, and Sophia met in their favorite spot—the treehouse. In the middle of the floor sat the old journal of softball secrets they found at the yard sale, waiting for them to dive in. They were eager to see what new lessons the book had for them.

"Are you ready to see what's next?" Ava asked, her eyes sparkling.

Sophia rubbed her tired eyes. "It's early, but I'm ready. This book has been cool so far."

"How about practice last night? Coach Moore was all about the energy meter," Ava said.

"The team was, too! Did you see how we hustled and stayed energized? Ava, you nailed it when you explained how we can choose our energy level. Giving 100% every pitch really made a difference." Zoe gave Ava a high-five.

"Did you see Mia's face light up when you said, 'Play every pitch like it's the first one of the game!'?" Addie asked.

"Sophia, I loved it when you said the number one goal for every player is to be 100% ready for the next pitch. That's how we win—one pitch at a time," Ava said.

"They totally got it! If we keep our energy up and stay Arrows-Out, instead of pouting after mistakes, we can beat anyone. I can't wait to see what Katie has for us next!" Zoe said.

Ava eagerly flipped through the pages, her eyes catching a new heading. "Hey, check this out." She read aloud.

**Keeping Your Cool: Dealing with Emotions and Bouncing Back from Tough Times.**

"It's about staying calm when you get nervous or mad during a game. It also talks about starting fresh when things go wrong. Look at this sentence—it says, **'You have to control your emotions before you can control how you play!'**"

The girls nodded, remembering the times when their emotions had taken over and how it felt to lose control.

Addie's eyes lit up. "This is exactly what I need! Before big games, I get too nervous, and if I make a mistake, I get too mad. My mom's always telling me to stop pouting."

Sophia frowned. "Same here! When I'm pitching and I get mad, my pitches go everywhere except where they're supposed to—across the plate."

Zoe nodded. "It's so hard to let go of errors. I keep thinking about them, get too emotional, and play worse."

Ava raised her eyebrows and said, "It says it's totally normal to feel nervous or mad during a game. Everyone feels it—even the best college players. They just know how to handle those feelings when they happen, so you shouldn't feel bad when those emotions happen. There's nothing wrong with that, but this journal can really help us be in control of our emotions."

Sophia blew out a breath. "Well, that's a relief!" She glanced at Zoe, who nodded.

Ava gave her friends an encouraging smile and kept reading. "There's a simple but powerful way to stay cool under pressure: deep breathing and the 3 Ts."

Addie's brow scrunched. "The 3 Ts?"

Ava glanced up. "Yeah, the 3 Ts. I'll get to that in a sec, but think about it. A little nervousness is fine, but when it takes over, everything gets harder."

Addie sighed. "I know exactly how that feels. Last game, I was so nervous when I batted. My stomach was full of butterflies, and my heart was pounding. It felt like everyone was staring at me. The pitcher threw three perfect pitches, and I didn't swing once. I was totally frozen."

"Addie, check this out," Ava said, still reading. "When you're too anxious, your muscles get tight, and your breathing gets fast and shallow. Your mind races with too many thoughts, making it hard to react to the next pitch."

"That's exactly what happened!" Addie quickly said. "So, what's the secret to calming down?"

Ava pointed to the page. "Here it is—it's called deep breathing."

"Deep breathing is a simple way to relax when those nerves kick in. It's easy to practice, and you'll get better each time."

Zoe jumped up. "Let's try it right now! Ava, show us what to do."

Ava grinned. "Okay, stand up and act like you're nervous. Breathe fast and shallow. Ready? Go!"

The girls giggled as they exaggerated their fast breathing, pretending to be nervous.

After a moment, Ava said, "Okay, stop! How did that feel? Relaxed?" She looked around, waiting for their reactions.

"No way! I felt jumpy, and my muscles were tight. I even felt kind of scared," Addie said. "It was just like that bad at-bat I told you about."

Ava continued, "Now, let's try deep breathing. Close your eyes, breathe in slowly through your nose, and count to four. Picture the air filling your belly like a balloon."

The girls followed along.

"Now, hold your breath for a few seconds. Then blow it out through your mouth. Imagine your worries flying away. Let your shoulders relax. Let's do it a few more times."

Ava smiled. "The book says, 'Pretend you're smelling a flower, then blow out candles on your birthday cake.'"

## A Correct Deep Breath

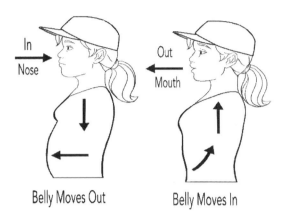

"When you're done, notice how you feel. Is your heart beating slower? Do you feel more relaxed?" Ava asked, glancing at each of them.

"I totally do!" Zoe said, nodding.

"Same here," Sophia added.

"I almost fell asleep," Addie joked.

Zoe nudged her, and the group burst out laughing.

Ava grinned. "See? It really works!"

Ava kept reading. "Deep breathing tells your body that everything's okay. It's a secret skill other players might not even know! Use it anytime you feel nervous—before a game, a test, or even a big presentation."

"Wow, I love that you can use it in a lot of ways," Zoe said.

"I could sure use deep breathing right before one of Mrs. Bowers' math tests," Addie joked.

Sophia glanced at her. "Yeah, no kidding."

Ava grinned. "Well, Mrs. Bowers' math tests aside, let's practice it every day and remind each other to use it during games."

The girls all nodded.

"But what about when you get mad or upset when things go wrong?" Sophia asked, scratching her head. "Like when you strike out, miss a play, or the ump makes a bad call?"

"Great question! When you get too mad, it only makes things worse. You lose focus on winning the next pitch, which is always the number one goal."

Addie jumped in. "Yeah, I've seen players get mad in games and then mess up again because they're still upset."

Zoe shook her head. "I can't stand it when our players get mad and throw their helmets or slam stuff down. It makes the everyone feel tense. It also makes our whole team look bad."

"When the other team sees you throw a tantrum, it makes them feel confident. They know they've got you. That's why it's so important to calm down fast. Let's see what the book says," Ava said.

She flipped the page. *"Dealing with Frustration and Anger,"* she read aloud.

"Softball's tough because everyone wants to be perfect. But no one is—not even the best college players. They still strike out, miss grounders, or walk batters. It's normal to get upset, but top players let it go quickly so they're ready for the next pitch. We can do that, too."

Sophia sighed. "But it's not always easy."

Ava nodded, still skimming the page. "Yeah, it's tough. But this book talks about something called a 'reset' that can help."

"What's a reset?" Zoe asked, tilting her head.

"What do you do when your computer or video game glitches?" Ava asked with a grin.

"I hit reset. Everything starts fresh, like nothing happened," Addie said, smiling confidently.

"Exactly! A reset lets you start fresh and forget the mistake. A great reset is called the 3 Ts," Ava said.

"The first T is '**Take a Deep Breath.**' Like we practiced earlier, deep breaths calm you down when you're frustrated. They slow your body and mind, helping you get back in control. Take as many as you need." She took a slow, deep breath.

Step 1. Take a Deep Breath

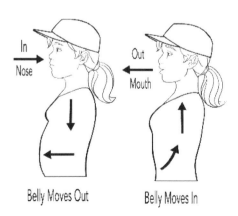

Ava held up two fingers. "The second T is '**Throw Away the Mistake.**' Do something physical to get rid of it, like squeezing dirt and tossing it away. As you do it, tell yourself the mistake is gone for good."

The girls leaned in, hanging on to every word.

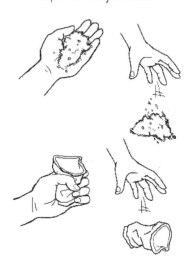

Step 2. Throw away the mistake

"Can pitchers do that, too? Like, after a bad pitch?" Sophia asked.

"Let's see." Ava scanned the page. "Pitchers can toss dirt, squeeze the rosin bag, wipe their foot on the rubber, or swipe their glove on their leg. It's all about starting fresh."

Addie jumped up, pretending to swing a bat. "What about hitters? What can we do after a bad at-bat?"

"Hitters need a reset, too," Ava said. "After a tough at-bat, you could crush a water cup like you're squashing your mistake and toss it in the trash. Or wipe off your bat before putting it away. That bad at-bat? Gone!"

"And the last T," Ava said, holding up three fingers again, "'**Tell Yourself Something Positive.**' After you throw away the mistake, remind yourself that you're a great player. Say something like 'I'm ready for the next play,' or 'I've got this!' It helps you stay confident and focused on just winning the next pitch."

Ava added, "Using the 3 Ts is better than moping, pouting, or throwing a tantrum. Those things just make you look bad and won't help your game. From now on, let's use the 3 Ts to reset every time something doesn't go right. Our goal? Getting really good at resetting and letting go of mistakes."

Ava smiled as she closed the journal and looked at each of them. "So, Sting, if we want to stay on top of our game, we need to control our emotions—and now we know the secret. Addie, can you remind us what we've learned?"

"Sure! I've got it all here," Addie said, scrolling through her tablet. "We learned a lot about handling our feelings today. For nerves, we take deep breaths—like smelling flowers and blowing out birthday candles. It calms us down, anytime, anywhere."

She continued, "For anger after mistakes, remember, nobody's perfect. Even the best players mess up. Reset with the 3 Ts: **Take a deep breath, toss the mistake away, and tell yourself something positive.** It's like resetting a video game—every pitch is a new chance to do something great. No moping. No pouting. No tantrums!"

Addie looked thoughtful. "Now we know how to handle those tough moments and stay cool under pressure."

The girls could see how these simple steps would help them shake off nerves and frustration, letting them play their best. As they kept talking, they circled back to how these skills could help in other parts of their lives, too.

"You know, just like Addie said earlier," Zoe said, "I get really nervous before big tests. My heart races, and my mind goes blank. I bet deep breathing could help with that, too."

Ava nodded. "Last week, I had to do a class presentation. I was so nervous I couldn't stop fidgeting. If I'd done deep breathing first, I would've felt way more confident."

Sophia added, "I don't mind presentations, but it's like Addie said with Mrs. Bowers' tests. I get so frustrated when I can't figure out a math problem. But instead of getting upset, I could use the 3 Ts to calm down and say, 'Reset. I can do this one step at a time.'"

Addie grinned at her friend. "Hey, you've got this one in the bag, Sophia. You too, Zoe. I'm done worrying about silly math tests."

With deep breathing and the 3 Ts of resetting, Ava, Zoe, Addie, and Sophia knew they could stay calm and focused, as long as they put their minds to the task. Even when things got tough, they had the power to stay in control and tackle anything.

Ava closed the book and skimmed her fingers over the old cover, wondering once again about its owner, Katie. What had become of her? Where was she today? If she were standing here with them, would she be proud of them for reading her book and taking her suggestions seriously?

**Solve These Mystery Questions!**

1. Show a friend or family member how to do deep breathing. Try teaching them the "smell the flowers, blow out the candles" method and see how it helps them feel relaxed. Did they like it?

2. Imagine you just made a mistake—describe exactly how would you use the 3 Ts to reset. Practice your 3 Ts during practice so they become automatic in games. Once you throw away the mistake, make sure it stays away!

3. For the last T, what are some positive things you can say to yourself after a mistake? Think of one or two sentences that you can remember and use next time you make a mistake.

## CHAPTER 5

# These Bulldogs Bite!

The sun was high in the cloudless sky, its bright rays gleaming off the metal bleachers. A warm breeze swept across the field and rustled the flags beyond the outfield fence. As game time approached, parents and fans buzzed with excitement. The Southport Sting players stretched and chatted, eager to get started.

The undefeated Boiling Springs Bulldogs warmed up along the left field line, their bright orange jerseys popping against the green grass. Bold black letters spelling "BULLDOGS" stretched across their chests like a warning sign to the Sting players.

The Sting charged onto the field, bursting with energy. Their warm-ups were sharp, every throw and catch smooth. As the home team, they stayed on the field, hearts racing as they took their positions.

The umpire's voice boomed, "Play ball!"

Asia Smith stepped in as the Bulldogs' leadoff hitter, a confident smirk on her face. Sophia stood tall in the circle, eyes locked on Hannah's sign. With a smooth wind-up, she let the ball fly, feeling the familiar tingling in her fingers as it left her hand.

The first pitch was a blur, straight down the middle. Asia gritted her teeth and swung hard, but her bat sliced through the empty air.

"Steeerike!" the umpire bellowed, his voice echoing above the crowd's buzz.

Sophia grinned as she caught the ball from Hannah. *I've got her*, she thought. After a foul ball, Sophia struck her out on a blazing fastball.

Sophia smiled. *What a start!* She snapped the ball into her mitt, her confidence growing. The next two batters didn't stand a chance.

Emma scooped up a slow grounder at first, while Zoe easily snagged a soft liner at shortstop, ending the inning.

The Sting sprinted toward the dugout, cleats kicking up dirt, eager for their turn at bat.

The Sting had strong hitters, but today, Amelia Johnson—the Bulldogs' ace pitcher—would be their real challenge. Each of Amelia's warm-up pitches echoed through the park, the pop of the ball in the mitt like firecrackers drawing everyone's eyes.

Addie silently watched from the dugout, biting her lip as her stomach twisted. *She throws the ball so fast! How can I hit her when I can't even see it?*

The first two Sting hitters struck out quickly, swinging at Amelia's blazing fastballs. But then, Hannah poked a bloop single to right field, breathing life into the inning. Ava stepped up and drilled a hard-hit single to left, setting off cheers from the Sting fans. With two outs and runners on first and second, Addie's heart raced. It was her turn.

Addie's breath quickened with every step to the plate, the knots in her stomach twisting tighter. She felt the weight of the moment. Slowly, she scanned the stands. The shouts of encouragement all blurred together—some for her, some for the Bulldogs' pitcher

Before stepping into the batter's box, Addie glanced down the third base line, looking to Coach Moore for reassurance.

"You got this. Just relax," Coach Moore called, giving her a small fist pump.

Addie nodded slightly, though her nerves didn't settle a bit.

Coach Moore's words barely registered. Addie's thoughts spun, fluttering like the butterflies in her stomach. *What if I strike out?* Addie swallowed hard, fighting the lump in her throat.

The first pitch zipped past her bat before she could even blink, but she swung anyway.

*Whoosh!*

*Wow, that was fast!* Addie's eyes widened in surprise.

"A little quicker, Addie!" Coach Moore shouted.

Addie's sweaty palms gripped the bat tighter. Her eyes flicked to the Bulldogs' dugout, where their players clapped and shouted, "You've got her, Amelia! Strike her out! She can't hit you!" The words stung, rattling her already shaky confidence.

*Maybe they're right. Maybe I can't hit her.*

Addie, her eyes wide, hoped the next pitch would be slower. But it wasn't. The next fastball was a blur, skimming the dirt for ball one. Addie barely saw it. Two more fastballs zipped by, luckily outside the strike zone.

*Whew! Those pitches flew by in a flash. It's 3 and 1. I hope she walks me,* Addie thought, feeling her nerves ease slightly. *I just won't swing, and maybe I can walk.*

The next pitch zipped into the catcher's mitt—another fastball, another strike. Addie's heart raced. *I can't strike out, not now!*

Addie stepped out of the batter's box, a part of her wishing she didn't have to step back in. The crowd's cheers echoed louder in her head. Addie rubbed her face slowly, her eyes darting all over the park.

The umpire motioned for her to get back into the batter's box. Addie's legs wobbled as she stepped in, every muscle tense. Three balls, two strikes—this was it.

*Don't strike out! Whatever you do, don't strike out!* Addie locked eyes with the Bulldogs' pitcher. Amelia scowled and nodded to her catcher.

*Oh boy.* Addie's stomach twisted into knots, like she was stuck at the top of a roller coaster, bracing for the drop.

Amelia hurled the ball, a laser zipping straight down the middle. Addie froze, her arms heavy like they couldn't move.

"Steeerike three!" the umpire shouted, turning and punching the air.

The Bulldogs' fans roared with cheers, their players sprinting off the field in celebration. Addie stood at home plate, her bat feeling like lead in her hands. Disbelief and shame twisted in her gut as she stared at the ground.

*What just happened? It was right down the middle!* Addie's mind spun. Her mouth hung open as her heart sank. She felt the sting of tears but blinked them away. Lowering her head, she dragged her feet as she trudged back to the bench.

"I should've swung. I don't know why I didn't... I just froze," Addie muttered to herself. "I totally blew it," she groaned, shaking her head.

Still replaying the strikeout in her mind, Addie grabbed her glove and trudged to second base, regret weighing down every step. "I had a perfect chance, and I just stood there like a statue," she grumbled, kicking the dirt.

"Addie! Addie!" Emma, the Sting's first baseman, called out, snapping Addie out of her thoughts.

Startled, Addie looked up as Emma's warm-up ball rolled past her. Addie finally grabbed the ball and made a half-hearted throw that barely reached Emma.

"C'mon, Addie! Get your head in the game!" Emma yelled, frustration clear in her voice.

Addie flinched but said nothing.

Emma fired another warm-up grounder to Addie. Addie stepped forward, reaching for the ball, but it skipped off the tip of her glove. Frustration boiling, she scrambled to grab it and angrily launched it toward first.

"Look out!" Emma shouted as Addie's throw veered off toward the Bulldogs' dugout.

Several Bulldogs jumped aside as the ball slammed into the cement wall, just missing them. Emma chased down the rolling ball and shot Addie a glare. Addie looked away, heat rising in her cheeks.

From across the field, Ava cupped her hands and yelled, "Addie, reset!"

Addie knew exactly what Ava meant—reset. She remembered what she'd learned from Katie's journal: **Softball is played one pitch at a time. The most important pitch is always the next one.** She had to let go of that strikeout.

Addie hit the reset button in her mind and put the 3 Ts into action. First, she took a slow, deep breath, feeling it fill her lungs and settle in her belly. She held it for a moment before blowing it out, letting the tension go with it.

Next, Addie bent down, grabbed a handful of dirt, squeezed it, then tossed it away as if she were throwing her strikeout into the trash.

*That strikeout is over. It's gone. I'm not thinking about it anymore. Time to play great defense,* she told herself.

Finally, she told herself positive things. "You'll get her next time. You're a good hitter, Addie. Now be quick as a cat at second base."

With her nerves fading and her mind clear, Addie crouched, ready, focusing on the next pitch. She wasn't thinking about the strikeout anymore—she was ready to react.

It was a good thing, too, because Harper Wilson, the Bulldogs' power-hitter, was up next. Harper had led her team in home runs last year—she was dangerous.

Harper strolled to the plate, tightened her batting glove, and whipped the bat through the air with hard practice swings. She dug her back foot into the dirt with determination. Sophia nodded at Hannah's sign, wound up, and fired her best fastball. The ball hissed as it cut through the air.

*Crack!*

A sharp line drive shot off Harper's bat, rocketing toward the gap between first and second. Addie dove to her right, stretched out, and snagged the ball just inches from the dirt. She crashed into the dirt, her body skidding across the field, but her glove stayed firmly closed around the ball.

"Out!" the umpire shouted.

The Sting's bench erupted with cheers, their voices echoing across the field. The fans buzzed with excitement as a small cloud of dust drifted their way. Harper shook her head in disbelief, clearly frustrated as she glared at Addie. The Bulldog hitter couldn't believe it—she had crushed that ball, but somehow, Addie had made the play.

"Nice job! Great catch!" Sophia said, grinning as Addie handed her the ball.

Addie smiled back, her confidence returning.

From the dugout, Coach Moore called out, "Way to go, Addie!"

Addie's heart swelled, a wide smile stretching across her face.

She brushed the dirt off her uniform and glanced at Ava who nodded and gave her a thumbs-up.

"Way to reset, Addie! You were ready for that one!" Ava shouted.

Addie smiled back, her heart lighter. *The reset worked,* Addie thought. *If I hadn't used the 3 Ts, I never would have made that play.*

The game stayed scoreless through four tense innings with Sophia matching Amelia pitch for pitch. But in the fifth inning, the tension rose. With two outs, Sophia gave up two sharp singles and then lost control, walking the next batter on four straight pitches. The bases were loaded, and the Bulldogs' fans roared louder than ever, their cheers rumbling through the stands.

Coach Moore called time and jogged out to the mound, her face calm as the infielders exchanged nervous glances. The girls gathered around Sophia, waiting for Coach's words.

"Okay, Sophia, you're going to get us out of this inning," Coach Moore said with a confident smile.

Sophia nodded, her nerves easing slightly.

"Remember, it's all about winning the next pitch. Just throw this one, then the next. One pitch at a time."

Coach Moore looked each player in the eye. "Girls, it's Arrows-Out time! No moping. No doubting. Now's the time to show your toughness. Make a play and we'll get out of this!"

The coach's words lit a spark, sending a surge of energy through the team.

*It's just like Katie's old book said,* Sophia thought. *Coach Moore believes the same thing, so it must be true.*

"One, two, three—Sting!" the team shouted in unison before sprinting back to their positions.

Kayla Smith, one of the Bulldogs' best hitters, came to the plate, her face set with fierce determination. She had already singled out Sophia earlier and looked confident.

Sophia knew she couldn't think about that. *Take your deep breath. One pitch at a time*, Sophia reminded herself. She wiped the sweat from her forehead, narrowing her focus on Hannah's mitt and tuning out the crowd's roar.

The umpire called, "Play ball!" and the crowd's buzz rose into a low rumble, anticipation thick in the air.

Kayla swung at the first pitch, sending a sharp line drive down the left field line. Just foul, as the ball hooked at the last second. Gasps rippled through the crowd. That was close to disaster for the Sting.

Sophia didn't flinch. She took another deep breath, zeroed in on her target, and fired her best fastball. Kayla swung with all her might, her bat whipping through the air.

*Whoosh!*

Strike two.

Hannah flashed the sign for a change-up. Sophia gave a quick nod. She wound up and sent the ball spinning and dancing toward the plate. Kayla swung too early. The ball landed softly in Hannah's mitt.

Strike three! Inning over!

The Bulldogs' fans groaned in disappointment as the Sting's side erupted in cheers, their players leaping in celebration. Addie sprinted over to Sophia. They smacked gloves as the rest of the team swarmed their pitcher.

Coach Moore was waiting as Sophia reached the dugout, her eyes gleaming with pride.

"Just win the next pitch, Coach. Win the next pitch!" Sophia grinned.

The Sting players' energy was at an all-time high. Coach Moore pointed to the energy meter on the wall, the arrow maxed out in the green.

"Now, let's get the bats going!" Coach Moore clapped. "You girls are great hitters. Let's show it and put some runs on the board!"

Fired up and ready, the Sting grabbed their bats and got to work.

Mia kicked off the rally with a solid single to left field. The next two batters followed her lead. Gracie showed patience at the plate, coaxing a rare walk from Amelia. Then, Hannah stepped up, hitting a soft infield single that barely stayed fair.

The bases were loaded. The noise from the crowd was at a fever's pitch. It was their chance to break the scoreless tie.

It was Ava's turn. Southport's clean-up hitter stood tall, her grip tightening on the bat as she took a deep breath. Ava thrived in moments like this—pressure, noise, and the game hanging in the balance.

Addie stood at the edge of the dugout, her eyes glued to Ava, her heart pounding. "You got this, Ava," Addie whispered to herself, crossing her fingers.

"She always looks so confident," Zoe said to Addie, her voice barely heard over the crowd noise.

Addie nodded, her eyes never leaving Ava.

"She's a great hitter. I bet Amelia's going to start her off with a change-up," Addie guessed.

"No way, she's gonna get a fastball," Zoe said, banging on a metal trash can loud enough to echo above the crowd noise.

Amelia wound up, her arm a tornado-like blur as she unleashed a fastball right down the middle. Ava knew it was a fastball, and she was ready for it.

*Crack!*

With a powerful swing, Ava sent the ball rocketing high into the sky. The crowd held its breath as all eyes followed the ball. Time seemed to crawl as the Bulldogs' left fielder sprinted back, her eyes locked on the ball until she suddenly froze. She was out of room. The softball vanished over the fence. Grand slam!

The Sting players burst from the dugout like it was the last day of school, jumping and screaming as they mobbed Ava at home plate.

With their confidence soaring and their mental toughness guiding them, the Sting played flawlessly for the rest of the game. Every throw was sharp, every swing was powerful, and each player knew they had their teammates' backs.

As the final out was made, the scoreboard flashed: Sting 4, Bulldogs 0.

The grand slam had changed the game, but it was their mental game that truly secured the victory. Focusing on winning the next pitch, resetting after mistakes, and lifting each other up made the difference.

As Addie walked off the field, she caught Ava's eye. Ava grinned.

"We did it," Addie said, the weight of the game lifting from her shoulders.

"Yeah, and we did it by winning the next pitch," Ava replied, smiling. "Katie was right. That's how you play the game."

Still buzzing with excitement, the Sting packed up their gear while chatting and laughing. Their hearts were full—not just because they won, but because they knew they had played their best, one pitch at a time.

*Wow, that was amazing. Thanks, Katie, whoever you are,* Ava thought. *I wish I could meet you to thank you in person for your wonderful advice.*

**Solve These Mystery Questions!**

1. How do you feel before a big game? What do you do to get ready?

2. What did Addie do after she struck out that helped her make the big catch?

3. How did Sophia stay focused with the bases loaded?

CHAPTER 6

# Focus Your Flashlight: Blocking Out Distractions

"Last night's game was wild!" Ava exclaimed, practically bouncing as she scrambled into the treehouse.

"It was! Katie's journal helped so much. I just wish I had remembered to breathe—I could feel my heart pounding when I stepped up to bat," Addie said, rubbing her face. "After I struck out, my brain felt like it was spinning, but your reminder to use the 3 Ts snapped me out of it."

"Yep! Your reset helped you make that awesome diving catch." Ava grinned.

"And remember how Coach kept shouting, 'Arrows-Out!'?" Zoe added.

"Yeah, Sophia, your mental game was amazing! You were so calm, taking deep breaths and playing one pitch at a time during that bases-loaded jam," Addie said.

"These mental game skills are seriously paying off, and we're only halfway through the book! I can't wait to learn more," Sophia said, her eyes gleaming.

## Focus Your Flashlight: Blocking Out Distractions

"What's next, Ava?" Zoe asked, stretching her neck to peek at the book.

"Let's see!" Ava said, smiling as she handed the worn journal to Addie. "Your turn. We're all ears!"

Addie giggled, grinning as she carefully turned the page. The paper crackled, and her eyes lit up as if she was about to share the world's biggest secret.

"Here we go: *'Dealing with Distractions.'*" Addie paused, glancing at the others to build suspense before reading further.

"Softball is a game of split-second reactions. **To play your best, you need to focus completely on your target right before every pitch.** When you're batting, your target is the pitcher's release point, right down by her knee. For fielders, it's the spot where the bat and ball meet at home plate. And pitchers? They're locked onto the catcher's mitt—nothing else."

Addie read on, "Anything that pulls your focus away from the target is a distraction. The more distractions, the slower your reactions!"

Addie paused. "Katie wrote a note in the margin: 'Before you read on, make a list of all the things that can distract you during a game.'" She looked up, gently closing the book.

"Let's do it! I'll write them down," Ava said, grabbing her notebook.

"The crowd, the other team's chants, and when Coach gives us a million instructions at once," Zoe blurted out, rolling her eyes.

"Those are good ones! What about bad calls or the weather? If it's blazing hot or freezing, or if the ump misses a call, my focus is toast," Sophia added.

"And here's a big one—my own thoughts!" Addie groaned. "When I step into the box against a tough pitcher, my mind races, and before I know it—whoosh—the ball's past me."

"Wow, there's so much that can distract you right before each pitch," Ava said.

Addie nodded and read aloud. "The key to playing great softball is learning how to block out all distractions. Imagine your focus is like a flashlight beam. Wherever it shines, that's where your mind goes. The trick? Aim it right where it matters—on the target, right before the pitch."

Ava looked thoughtful. "Ah, so we can control our focus by aiming our flashlight where it matters instead of letting our minds wander?"

"Yep, you're the one holding the flashlight." Addie laughed, pretending to shine it around the room.

"But how do we actually do that?" Zoe asked, leaning in. "Blocking everything out in a big game is so tough."

Addie tapped the page like she'd just found buried treasure. "Katie says if you get distracted, there are three quick steps to get your focus back. Ready?"

"More than ready," Zoe murmured.

She turned the book so the girls could read, their eyes widening with excitement.

*Focus Your Flashlight: Blocking Out Distractions*

> **Step one:** Pay attention to where your flashlight is pointing. If it's not locked on to the next pitch, go to step two.
>
> **Step two:** Say "STOP!" in your head. It snaps your focus back to where it belongs.
>
> **Step three:** Pick a phrase that snaps your mind back to the game, like "Next pitch," "Focus," or "Reset." Choose one that pulls your focus back to the target.

"So, first you check where your mind is at. If it's not on the pitch, you say 'stop' and hit it with your refocus phrase," Ava explained.

"That makes so much sense! If you don't catch it, you'll stay distracted," Zoe said, her eyes lighting up as she understood.

"It's harder than it sounds." Addie sighed. "Has your flashlight ever gotten stuck on your own thoughts? Sometimes my brain is racing, and I don't even see the pitch coming. No wonder I struck out twice against the Bulldogs," she groaned.

Sophia frowned. "Same here. When I was pitching, the crowd was so loud I couldn't block them out. My flashlight was stuck on the noise, not on Hannah's mitt. My pitches went everywhere."

"But now you know—you're the one in control of your focus," Ava said with a grin.

"From now on, I'm sticking to those steps to get my focus back," Zoe said, her eyes brimming with determination.

Addie paused before turning the next page. "Whoa, check this out! There's a game to help us practice staying focused on a target!"

The girls leaned in as Addie read aloud. "It's called a concentration grid. There are twenty-five numbers scattered around. You have to find them in order from 1 to 25 using your finger. See how many you can get in 30 seconds and then try to find all of them as fast as possible."

*Focus Your Flashlight: Blocking Out Distractions*

## Concentration Grid

| 12 | 06 | 20 | 11 | 08 |
|----|----|----|----|----|
| 25 | 13 | 09 | 21 | 19 |
| 02 | 10 | 23 | 01 | 16 |
| 04 | 17 | 03 | 24 | 07 |
| 15 | 05 | 18 | 14 | 22 |

She continued, "Sounds easy, right? But here's the tricky part—there'll be distractions. You'll hear noises, and even your own thoughts will mess with you. Just keep your flashlight on the number. Let's see if you can stay focused."

Zoe grinned. "This is just like a real game! There are distractions everywhere. If we block them out, we'll do better."

The girls giggled, ready for the challenge. Ava went first, her eyes darting across the grid like a detective. She quickly found the first few numbers, but Zoe's tapping foot threw her focus off.

"Ugh, I lost focus! Twelve!" Ava groaned, slumping in frustration.

Zoe took her turn, determined to beat Ava's score. She was on a roll, but then her own thoughts crept in. *Hurry! I've got to beat her*, she thought. Her heart raced, and panic set in, making her lose focus.

"I only got ten. You got me, Ava. I was doing fine until my own thoughts tripped me up." Zoe giggled. "My flashlight was in my head, not on the numbers. You probably saw my eyeballs light up like a Christmas tree!"

The girls burst out laughing.

Ava nodded, still grinning. "See? That's what happens when your flashlight drifts off target."

Zoe rolled her eyes. "Yeah, yeah, rub it in."

Ava smirked. "Well, it's thanks to your foot tapping that I didn't get through it all."

*Focus Your Flashlight: Blocking Out Distractions*

Zoe was about to reply when Sophia held up her hands between her friends and said, "Speaking of distractions, let's not let an argument get us off topic. Come on, girls."

Sophia added, "Yeah, let's refocus our flashlight."

The tension broke, and they all laughed.

"Sorry about that," Ava said, looking at Zoe.

"No worries. They're right, though. Let's just get back to it, huh?"

Ava winked. "You got it! Now, let's keep practicing this so we get better at focusing, and then we can use it in games."

Zoe nodded. "Next time I'm up to bat, and the other team's chanting, I'll lock my flashlight only on her release point. Everything else will fade away."

"And if my focus slips while I'm pitching, I'll use my refocus phrase, 'Hit your spot,' to bring my flashlight back to the catcher's mitt," Sophia said, gripping an imaginary ball in her hand.

Addie's eyes lit up. "Wait, this isn't just for softball! We can use this at school, too. If we get distracted while studying, we can pull our flashlight back to what we need to focus on instead of letting our minds wander."

"Great point, Tech Girl." Ava grinned. "This proves concentration's not about trying harder—it's all about aiming your flashlight at what really matters. Now we know exactly how to do it!"

They all high-fived.

*I wonder if you ever allowed distractions, even arguing with your friends and teammates, to get in the way, Katie,* Ava thought as she gazed out the window.

**Solve These Mystery Questions!**

1. Many things can distract you during a game. What distracts you the most?

2. What are the three steps you can use to get your focus back if you're distracted during a game?

3. Play the concentration game with a parent or a friend. Use the grids in the back of the book. Set a timer for 30 seconds and see who can get the most numbers. Then, time each other as you try to find all 25! Write your personal records here.

CHAPTER 7

# Talk Like a Champ: Make Your Mind Your MVP

On a cool Saturday afternoon, Ava, Sophia, Zoe, and Addie huddled in Ava's cozy living room, their heads bent over the book of softball secrets. Ava's cat, Oliver, brushed against their legs, meowing for attention, but they hardly noticed. With an annoyed flick of his tail, Oliver wandered away.

"This one looks big," Ava said, her voice serious. "It's about self-talk."

"Self-what?" Sophia asked, scratching her head.

"It's how we talk to ourselves during games," Ava explained. "The journal says we all have two voices. Your Inner Coach, who builds you up, and your Inner Critic, who brings you down."

"I don't like the sound of the Inner Critic," Sophie admitted with a frown.

"Well, I'm sure Katie has ways to help with that." Ava leaned in closer and read aloud. "Your thoughts are powerful. What you tell yourself can either make you stronger or weaker. If you keep thinking, 'I can't do this,' you'll start to believe it."

Addie nervously twisted a strand of hair. "It happens to me when I'm batting. If I strike out, that voice sneaks in and says, 'You'll strike out again.' It's like a sneaky thief stealing my confidence," she said quietly.

"Same here," Zoe admitted, her shoulders sagging. "I try to push those thoughts away, but they just take over. What are we supposed to do about it?"

Ava glanced down at the book. "Negative self-talk happens to everybody. Even top college players on TV hear that doubting voice at first. But they've learned self-talk tricks to stay confident. This chapter explains how. See? I told you Katie wouldn't let us down."

"I never realized that," Zoe said, her eyes widening. "So, what you tell yourself is what you start believing?"

Ava turned the book, pulling it closer so everyone could read the next part.

**Self-Talk is a Choice.** You get to decide what to say to yourself. Negative thoughts will automatically appear out of nowhere, but it's your choice whether to listen or replace them.

**Catch and Switch:** If you catch yourself thinking something negative, you can switch it to something positive. It's like changing the channel from a sad movie to a fun one. Most players don't realize they have this power, but anyone can use it. After a mistake, instead of saying, 'I'm terrible,' say, 'I'll get the next one!' Those words build your confidence and get you ready for the next play.

"I tried that," Ava said. "I missed an easy catch and thought, 'Ava, you're awful.' But then I flipped it. I told myself, 'You're the best fielder on the field.' Right away, I felt more confident. And guess what? The next fly ball? Caught it!"

Addie tapped her head. "I just figured out something. Changing your self-talk helps you play with an Arrows-Out attitude."

Ava smiled and said, "Great point, Addie. Saying things like 'I'm terrible' or 'I can't' are Arrows-In words. They make you feel sorry for yourself instead of pointing your arrows back at the game."

Sophia nodded. "And remember, positive self-talk keeps your energy meter in the green."

"Oh, now it all makes sense," Zoe said, her eyes lighting up. "All these mental game skills are connected. Each one makes the others stronger."

The girls nodded, and Ava flipped the page. "Look at this—another awesome idea!"

**Say What You Want to Happen, Not What You Fear:** Focus on what you want to do, not on what you're scared of. For example, instead of saying, 'Don't miss the ball,' say, 'Make a great play.' Your mind believes what you tell it. You'll see yourself succeeding instead of failing!

"This tip is a total game-changer, especially when things get tough," Ava said. "Close your eyes and imagine you're walking through the cafeteria, holding your lunch tray. If you think, 'Don't drop it,' or 'Don't embarrass yourself,' what picture pops into your mind?"

"Splat! All over the floor!" Sophia shouted, throwing her arms wide.

The girls burst out laughing.

"When you focus on what scares you, you picture it happening. That just makes you more nervous," Ava explained. "And less confident."

"Picture this. You're up to bat, bases loaded, two outs. If you say, 'Don't strike out,' how would that make you feel? What picture pops into your head?" she asked, glancing around the room.

"That's easy! I've totally done that," Addie blurted out. "I pictured myself striking out, and it made me even more nervous!"

"We've all been there, right?" Zoe said, looking at her friends.

They all nodded.

"Now, flip it. Instead of thinking, 'Don't strike out,' tell yourself, 'Hit the ball hard!' What do you see in your head?" Ava asked.

"I'd see myself smashing it. I'd feel strong instead of nervous," Zoe said, pretending to take a big swing.

Ava tapped her forehead with her finger. "Exactly! When you focus on what you want, it changes the movie in your mind."

Ava continued, "And this isn't just for softball. It works for other sports, too, like shooting a free throw in basketball or serving in volleyball. You've got to picture yourself nailing it, not messing up."

She paused, looking up. "If your dad plays golf and thinks, 'Don't hit the ball into the water,' what do you think he pictures? And what usually happens? Splash! Right into the water!"

The girls giggled.

Zoe grinned to herself. *I can't wait to tell my dad this tip. He loves golf, and this could totally help him. He'll love it.*

Sophia's eyes lit up. "Does this work for pitchers, too?"

"Sure! Imagine you've got a 3-0 count on a batter. You need to throw a strike. If your self-talk keeps saying, 'Don't walk her,' how would that feel? What would you see?"

"That's easy!" Sophia exclaimed. "That happened to me last game. It was 3-0, and I started stressing out thinking I'd walk her. In my head, I saw my pitch missing before I even threw it. And guess what? Ball four."

"Okay, Sophia picture that same 3-0 count, but this time you say, 'Throw strikes,' or 'Hit your spot.' Wouldn't that change what you see and feel?"

"Yep! I'd be totally focused and feel like I'm in control out there. I'd see that pitch going right where I wanted it to go," Sophia replied, flexing her wrist like she was throwing a fastball.

"So, girls, before each pitch, say what you want to happen, not what you're worried about. Got it?" Ava asked.

"Got it!" the girls said together.

**Avoid Those Confidence-Killing Words:** Phrases like 'I can't' or 'I'm not' instantly make you doubt yourself. That doesn't help you play better. Top players avoid these phrases, and you can, too. Here are more examples:

- It's no use.
- I won't be able to do it.

- I stink.
- We can't win.
- I should just give up.

"That's such a cool idea," Zoe said, nodding.

**Use Your Own Power Phrases:** Choose a short phrase or two that pumps you up. These are your secret phrases to quickly boost your confidence. It could be something like "I'm unstoppable" or "I've got this." Use these phrases every day, both on and off the field, to build confidence. You can even write one on your glove as a reminder.

"I'm definitely using a power phrase," Sophia said, nodding. "How about 'Nobody better!'? That'll fire me up." She pumped her fist, grinning.

"I'm going with 'You're the toughest two-strike hitter ever!'" Addie said.

"Mine's going to be 'It's crushing time.' It'll remind me of all the times I've ripped the ball," Ava said with a huge smile.

"These tips are awesome. Let's see what's next," Zoe said eagerly.

**Treat Yourself Like Your Best Friend:** After a mistake, talk to yourself the way you would talk to your best friend. You wouldn't tell your friend they're awful just because they made a mistake.

"Imagine your friend just struck out. What would you say to her?" Ava asked.

"If Zoe struck out, I'd tell her she's a good hitter, and she'll get her next time," Sophia said quickly.

"Hey, Sophia!" Zoe protested, making a face. "You didn't have to use me as an example."

The girls laughed.

"Why would you say something nice to her?" Ava asked, tilting her head.

"I'd want her to stay confident. That way, she'll play her best the rest of the game," Sophia explained.

Ava raised her eyebrows. "So, you wouldn't say, 'You're terrible!' or 'You can't hit!' or 'You should just stop playing softball'?"

The girls shook their heads, giggling at the thought.

"You wouldn't, but I bet you've said mean things like that to yourself after striking out or messing up," Ava said.

The girls ducked their heads, mumbling about their own bad self-talk.

"Your words are powerful. They can lift you up or drag you down. Sometimes we're too hard on ourselves, and it doesn't help us win the next pitch. Don't say anything to yourself that you wouldn't say to your best friend."

"Wow, that totally makes sense," Addie said. "Telling yourself you're terrible after a mistake doesn't make you better—it just crushes your confidence."

Ava flipped the page, her gaze landing on a yellowed headline. "Whoa, look! It's a newspaper clipping! Katie played for Southport. They won the 1983 Southport City Championship. There's no team picture, but it's definitely another clue."

## Southport Sports
*August 17, 1983*

### SOUTHPORT WINS CITY SOFTBALL CHAMPIONSHIP!

Addie rubbed her forehead. "The Southport City Championship is the biggest game of the year in Southport, and it's always for 12U."

Addie flipped back to the doodles on the first page of Katie's journal. "Wait, I got it!" she exclaimed, her eyes lighting up. "February 15, 1971—that's her birthday. She turned twelve in 1983!"

"Nice work, Sherlock!" Sophia giggled as she gave Addie a playful nudge. "You're becoming quite the detective."

Ava pointed to the journal. "Look under the clipping. There's a note."

Ava squinted as she read aloud. "Remember, your mind can be your best friend or your worst enemy—it's up to you. During the 1983 Championship, we were down by three runs, and my self-talk kept saying, 'Don't strike out. Don't strike out.' But then I caught myself and changed it to 'Rip the ball,' 'The pitcher's scared of you,' and 'You're a great hitter.' I smashed a home run, and we came back to win — Diamond Girl."

"So, Katie switched her self-talk, and it worked," Sophia said, her eyes glued to the note.

"She must've been a really smart player. No wonder she was MVP," Addie said, eyes wide. "And get this, her nickname was Diamond Girl, just like we thought!"

The girls studied the clipping and the note closely. Their imaginations drifted back to that big day in 1983.

"Well, Katie, or should I say Diamond Girl, proved that positive self-talk really works! Let's make sure we use it every day from now on," Ava said with a grin.

"Deal!" the girls shouted, their excitement overflowing.

The next day at practice, the Sting girls were ready to put their new self-talk strategies to the test. Zoe, usually the team jokester, got serious for once and whispered, "I am confident," as she stepped into the batter's box. Sophia, always laser-focused, took a deep breath and repeated, "I'm strong under pressure," before delivering a perfect pitch. Addie, who tended to overthink, concentrated on her breathing and reminded herself, "I've got this," whenever she felt anxious.

Armed with their new self-talk skills, the girls felt ready for anything.

As the Sting girls headed home, their thoughts drifted back to the mystery of Katie. Who was this player from forty years ago who had mastered these mental game skills? The girls were more determined than ever to learn more about "Diamond Girl."

## Solve These Mystery Questions!

1. What is self-talk, and how can changing it help you play better? What are some steps you can take to turn negative self-talk into positive self-talk?

2. Write three things you'd say to a friend who struck out to help them feel better. Now, write three things you've said to yourself after striking out. Are they the same? How can you start talking to yourself the way you would to your friend?

3. Why is it important to say what you want to happen, like "Hit the ball hard," instead of focusing on what you're afraid of, like "Don't strike out"?

## CHAPTER 8

# Stop Thinking So You Can Start Hitting!

The next morning, the girls gathered at the batting cage, excitement buzzing as they waited for Ava to share a new mental game secret.

"Girls, last night I read the next part of Katie's journal. I thought this was the perfect place to teach what I learned to you. It's about using a new type of pre-pitch routine. It's very important to learn this if you want to be a great hitter," Ava said, her voice full of energy.

Addie glanced at the others. Their eyes were wide, locked on Ava as they soaked in every word.

Ava continued, "Softball pitches come at you fast. You only have a split second to decide whether to swing. But if you're thinking about the crowd, the other team, or worrying about missing the ball, your brain gets too distracted. You won't be able to react to the pitch in time. The best hitters are the ones who learn to turn off their thoughts before the pitch."

Ava grabbed her bat and crouched. "Picture this: You're at the plate, and your mind races with all kinds of thoughts. Before you know it, the ball zooms past you. It's just a blur."

"But how do you stop thinking so much? There's always so much going on," Addie asked, lifting her bat. "The coach is shouting. I hear my parents and the other team chanting. And I can't stop talking to myself. My brain's on overload! And, with two strikes, it gets even worse."

"There's a special kind of pre-pitch routine that turns off all your thinking right before the pitch," Ava said, smiling.

"What's a pre-pitch routine?" Zoe asked.

"A pre-pitch routine is something you do before every pitch. We all have little routines—like taking a certain number of swings or fixing our batting glove. They help calm us down, but they don't turn off all the stuff going on in your head. Katie's secret pre-pitch routine does that for us. Not many players our age know about it."

"Okay, let's hear it," Zoe said.

Ava leaned in and held up four fingers. "The routine has four simple steps to shut off your thoughts and lock in on the pitch. The better you get at using this exact pre-pitch routine, the better hitter you'll be."

"That sounds cool! Show us how it works," Zoe said.

Ava stepped forward, pretending to walk up to the plate. With a determined look, she gripped her bat like she was about to hit a home run. "Okay, here's how to do the perfect pre-pitch routine."

Zoe and the others moved in closer. Ava was the best hitter on the team, and when she spoke, everyone paid attention.

"First," Ava said, "before you step into the batter's box, check with your third-base coach for signs." She pointed at an imaginary coach. "This is when you think. What does your coach want? What's the game situation? What pitch are you hoping for? Make your plan, but remember—this is the only time to think."

The girls nodded.

"Now, the next three steps are where the magic happens," Ava continued. "These steps help you lock in on the ball from the moment it leaves the pitcher's hand all the way to your bat."

"Step two is huge. We all get nervous when we bat, right? This is how you fix that. Before every pitch, take a deep breath, just like Katie showed us."

Zoe's eyes lit up. "Hey, I saw you doing that breathing thing last game!"

### Step 2. Take a Deep Breath

In — Nose

Out — Mouth

Belly Moves Out       Belly Moves In

"Yep, I do that before every pitch—breathe in through my nose and out through my mouth. I even let my shoulders relax when I do it." Ava showed them, taking a slow, deep breath in, then letting it out calmly.

Ava added, "If you're still nervous, it's fine to take a few more breaths. Sometimes I take two or three. Just breathe slow—no rush."

"Can we try the first two steps now? I want to make sure I get them right," Sophia asked eagerly.

"Sure!" Ava said. The girls lined up, each pretending to step up to the plate. They glanced at their imaginary third-base coach, then took a deep, steady breath, just like Ava had shown them.

Ava watched them, pride shining in her eyes. "Great job, everyone! How do you feel?"

Addie, who had been fidgeting earlier, now smiled. "I feel a lot more relaxed. My mind isn't racing like before."

"Good!" Ava said. "Step three is super important—maybe the most important. It's the real secret to turning off your thinking, and that's *exactly* what you want."

"Now, watch this," Ava said, holding up her bat. "Pick a tiny spot on your bat—this is your special 'focus point.' It's like a magic switch that turns off all the racing thoughts in your head. This is important because you can't be thinking and trying to hit at the exact same time."

She pointed to a tiny scratch on her bat and focused her eyes. "It can be anything—a scratch, a letter, a little design—whatever stands out to you. Look at it closely, like you're seeing it for the very first time. *Notice every tiny detail.* When you do that, nothing else matters. It's just you and that spot."

"Sounds, uh…interesting," Sophia said with uncertainty in her voice.

### Step 3. Study Focal Point

"Well, let's try it out then," Ava said, encouraging the girls.

Each girl grabbed her bat, found a focus point, and studied it closely.

Ava's voice broke the silence. "Did your thoughts disappear? Did your mind get quiet?"

"Wow, sure did!" Sophia broke the silence. "I had my doubts, but you were right, or should I say that Katie was right?"

They laughed.

"Yes, it totally worked!" Zoe said, grinning. "I wasn't thinking about anything. I even forgot where I was. All my focus was on that little spot."

Ava's eyes lit up. "Exactly! Your eyes were like that small flashlight beam we talked about before. They zeroed in on your spot. Doing that gets your brain ready for total concentration right before each pitch. Use the same focus point every time."

"Now, for the last step. Move your eyes from the focus point directly to the pitcher's release point—that spot by her leg where the ball comes out. If you only look at the release point, you'll see the ball a split second earlier and react faster. I like to think of it like I'm playing a video game, waiting for the ball to pop out."

Step 4. Only Look at the Release Point

Zoe furrowed her brow, thinking. "So, I just look at the release point? Not at the pitcher's face or anywhere else?"

"Exactly!" Ava said confidently. "If you look anywhere else, you'll get distracted. Picture your eyes are like a laser beam moving from the spot on your bat to the release point. You'll track the pitch better from her hand. If it's not a strike, let it go. If it is—smash it!"

"Won't it take too long to do all four steps?" Zoe asked, frowning.

"Nope! Practice it enough and you'll switch off your thoughts faster than you can turn off a light. No more distractions—not the crowd, not the other team, nothing."

Addie swung her bat slowly, following Ava's steps. "You do your routine, and then it's just you and the ball—bam!"

The girls nodded.

Eager to try what they learned, the girls tested their new pre-pitch routine in the batting cage. They set up the pitching machine, and the girls lined up to take turns.

"Remember what we talked about," Ava said as she stepped into the cage first. "Focus on your routine—no thinking, just you and the pitch."

Ava followed the steps just as she had explained. She checked with the coach, took a deep breath, locked her eyes on the focus point on her bat, and then her eyes went right out to where the ball would come out of the machine. The pitch came in fast, but Ava was ready. She swung smoothly and smacked a screaming line drive into the back of the net.

"Nice one, Ava!" Zoe cheered from the side, clearly impressed.

Zoe stepped up next.

"Since we're learning, take your time," Ava said. "You'll know you're doing it right when you react to the pitch without thinking about it."

Zoe nodded and carefully followed each step. When the pitch came, she hit a solid liner. She repeated the steps slowly, smashing one ball after another.

"Wow, that was awesome!" Zoe said, her excitement bubbling over. "I could see the seams on the ball way earlier, and I followed the ball all the way to my bat. My thoughts didn't get in the way—I was just seeing the ball and reacting. I love this! I'm definitely going to practice and use it in games!"

Addie watched closely. When her turn came, she felt confident. She followed the routine just like Ava and Zoe. The ball zipped out of the machine, but Addie was calm and focused. Her swing was quick, and the ball shot off her bat like a rocket. Swing after swing, she kept ripping the ball.

"That was awesome!" Addie said, hopping out of the cage. "This no-thinking secret is a game-changer!"

The girls were hitting better than ever. Zoe nudged Ava, grinning widely. "Look at us! We're crushing line drives!"

"This new routine is making a big difference," Ava said proudly. "It's already helping us become better hitters. I'll teach it to the rest of the team."

The girls practiced for another hour before it was time to leave.

Ava waved them in for a quick huddle. "I'm so proud of us! We'll keep practicing this routine until it becomes automatic in games. Right before the pitch, no thinking—just reacting." Ava added, "Before we go, here's the last thing Katie wrote: '**The better you get at turning off your thoughts, the better hitter you'll become.**'"

The Sting girls were buzzing with excitement. Could this new routine really make them unstoppable? They couldn't wait to find out.

*Wow, Katie, you almost seem too good to be true,* Ava thought, watching her friends grinning. *Could it really be this easy?*

## Solve These Mystery Questions!

1. Ava tells the girls that you can't be thinking when you're trying to see the pitch coming out of the pitcher's hand. She teaches them a great pre-pitch routine to help turn off thinking and just react. Write the steps and explain why each step is important.

2. Ava talked about using a focus point, like a spot on your bat. Get your bat and write down what you will use. Make sure it is tiny so you can study the details.

3. After you look at the focus point, it is important to look straight out at the release point. Practice at home by studying your focus point and then looking at something small far away, like a doorknob or spot on a tree. It could be anything. How did you feel when you looked at the imaginary release point? Was your focus sharper? Keep practicing this!

CHAPTER 9

# The Secret Skill: Seeing It Before You Do It

All three phones buzzed at once. A message from Addie lit up their screens. "Meet me at the Southport Library ASAP! Big news! Don't forget Katie's journal!"

The girls hurried to the library, eager to find out what was so important. Addie waved them over with a big grin as they walked in.

"What's the big news, Tech Girl? You sounded pretty excited," Ava said, sliding into her seat.

Zoe and Sophia exchanged curious looks, just as eager to hear what Addie had to say.

"Want to know who Katie is?" Addie teased, her voice playful.

"Yeah, spill it!" Ava said, eyes wide with excitement.

"And how did you figure it out?" Sophia blurted impatiently.

"Remember the clues? Her name's Katie, her nickname was Diamond Girl, and she played for Southport in the 1983 City Championship," Addie said. "And with that doodle, we figured out she was born in '71."

"Yeah, keep going," Zoe said, her eyebrows raised.

"I checked the doodle page again and noticed this," Addie said, pointing to a small sketch.

"It hit me—it stands for Southport Middle School! I knew this library had old yearbooks going back to the '70s. Are you ready for this?"

Addie grabbed the yearbook from beside her and flipped to a marked page. The girls gasped.

"It's their softball team! Did you find Katie?" Ava asked, heart racing.

"I did! She's right here," Addie said, pointing to a girl in the second row, second from the left. "Her name's Katie Parker."

"Whoa!" they all gasped at the same time.

"Nice work, Tech Girl! You nailed it. Katie Parker—that's her!" Sophia said, pointing to the picture.

The girls were still buzzing with excitement when Ava said, "Now that we know who Katie is, let's check out the next skill from the journal."

"I already read it, and it's awesome! I made copies for everyone," Addie said, pulling a stack of papers from her bag. "It's all about visualization. Let's dive in!"

The girls nodded eagerly, grabbed their copies, and started reading.

* * *

**Visualization**

Visualization is when you close your eyes and picture yourself doing something perfectly, just the way you want. You add sounds, smells, the way your body moves, and feel the excitement. It's like a super cool daydream—and you're the star! But it's more than daydreaming. It's a powerful mental tool called visualization.

Let's say you want to hit a line drive. Close your eyes and picture the pitcher winding up. Watch the ball zoom toward you as your bat swings perfectly. Hear the crack of the bat and see the ball rocket over the outfielder's head. Your teammates cheer as you race to first base. The more details you imagine—like the crack of the bat or the dirt under your feet—the better it works!

Now, picture a hot summer day, and the game is tied. The bases are loaded with two outs. You're on the field when the batter rips a line drive to your left. You dive and make the perfect catch. Feel the ball smack into your glove. Hear the roar of the crowd as they leap to their feet. You can almost taste the sweat on your lip as you run off the field.

When you picture yourself doing something great, it's like practicing for real. Your brain doesn't know if what you're imagining is real or not! This builds your confidence and makes it more likely to happen just like that in a real game.

Visualization really works! It's used by professional and Olympic athletes in all sports. It's an easy skill to learn and use. You can do it anywhere—on the bus, before bed, or even on the ride to the game!

**How to Visualize**

Visualization is easy, and the more you practice, the better you'll get. Like anything in softball, it takes practice. Here's how to do it:

1. **Find a Quiet Spot:** Go somewhere you won't be interrupted—like your room, the backyard, or a quiet corner on the field.

2. **Close Your Eyes:** Close your eyes and take a few deep breaths. This helps you relax and stay focused.

3. **Imagine a Scene:** Picture something you want to practice—hitting, pitching, or fielding. Add as many details as you can.

4. **Add Feelings:** Imagine what it feels like in that moment—your heart racing, your muscles ready. The more you can feel it, the better. What emotions are running through you?

5. **Use All Your Senses:** It's not just about seeing. Hear the crack of the bat, smell the fresh-cut grass, and feel the dirt under your feet. Using all your senses makes visualization stronger.

6. **Practice Makes Progress:** Try to visualize before every practice, game, or even just once a day. The more you do it, the stronger your brain's "superpower" gets.

## Visualization in Action: How to Use it in Games

1. **Hitting:** Picture yourself up to bat. The pitcher's ready, and you step into the batter's box. She winds up, and you lock in on the ball as it leaves her hand. You see it clearly and swing. Feel your bat vibrate as the ball flies into the outfield. The crowd cheers, and excitement rushes through you as you sprint to first base. Visualizing this before your at-bat teaches your brain what to do. It helps you feel more confident and ready to hit.

2. **Pitching:** If you're a pitcher, visualizing can help you stay calm and focused. Close your eyes and imagine yourself in the pitching circle. Grip the ball, feeling the seams under your fingers. Lock in on your catcher's target. Now, picture yourself throwing the perfect pitch. The ball spins just right, heading exactly where you aimed. The batter swings and misses! Visualizing this makes you feel more in control and confident on the mound.

3. **Fielding:** Picture yourself at shortstop with a runner on second. The ball's coming toward you, and you're ready. You scoop it up and throw hard to first base. The first baseman snags the ball, and the runner is out! Visualizing this play helps you stay ready when it happens in the game.

4. **Laying Down the Perfect Bunt:** Bunting under pressure is tough, especially when it's crunch time. That's where visualization comes in. You're at the plate, and you've finished your pre-pitch routine. The pitcher gets set to throw. As she releases the pitch, you calmly square up to bunt. You're holding the bat just right, and you see the ball coming right down the middle. You gently "catch" the ball with the bat, like it's part of you, almost like a glove. Feel the soft

thud as the ball meets the bat, laying down a perfect bunt that rolls smoothly, just out of reach. A huge grin spreads across your face as you sprint to first base. You're like the world's greatest bunter, and no one can stop you. Picture this scene again and again, and you'll feel more relaxed and in control when it's time to bunt.

Visualization isn't just for softball—you can use it anywhere. Whether you're giving a speech in class, acting in a school play, or playing another sport, visualization helps calm your nerves and build confidence.

* * *

Zoe looked up from her paper, eyes wide with surprise. "Wow, I never thought of using my imagination like this. It's like practicing without even swinging a bat."

Addie nodded. "Yeah, I like how you use all your senses to make it feel real. I bet it'll be fun, too!"

Sophia grinned. "I'm totally trying this. It'll help me before our next game. I always get nervous when I pitch. But if I see myself throwing strikes before the game, I'll feel way more confident."

Addie rubbed her chin. "It's not just for softball. Just like with the other tools we've learned, we can use it in other parts of our lives, too, like school. Remember those math tests?"

Zoe laughed. "Do I ever!"

"I'll use it in basketball and volleyball, too! This will be a total game-changer for all of us," Ava said, nodding seriously. "Let's all agree to practice visualization every day."

Addie sat quietly, her eyes closed, deep in thought.

Sophia nudged Addie. "What are you doing?"

"I was just visualizing all of us… visualizing."

The girls giggled, but quickly quieted down when they remembered they were in the library.

It was a big day for the Sting. Not only did they discover who Katie was, but they also learned another great mental game skill to help them play their best.

**Solve These Mystery Questions!**

1. Olympic and pro athletes use visualization. What are suggestions from the chapter that can help you make your visualization stronger?

2. What are the five senses you can use when visualizing, and why is it important to include all of them?

3. Practice visualizing for 5-10 minutes every day. Try to make it feel real.

4. Besides softball, where else can you use visualization?

CHAPTER 10

# No More Doubt: How to Play with Confidence

The morning sun streamed through the branches of the big oak tree, casting stripes of light and shadow on the grass. A soft breeze lifted strands of the girls' hair as Ava, Addie, Sophia, and Zoe sat cross-legged under the tree. They had reached the last chapter of Katie's journal.

Ava flipped through the worn pages until her eyes brightened. "Found it!" she said, tapping the bold title: *Playing with Confidence*.

Zoe leaned in, peeking over Ava's shoulder. "I need this," she muttered. "Confidence is hard. One mistake and it's like all the good plays I've made just vanish." She sighed.

Sophia nodded, her brows furrowed. "I know what you mean," she whispered. "It's hard to stay confident after messing up, especially in a big game." She exchanged a knowing look with Zoe.

Addie grinned. "Maybe this chapter will show us how to stay confident when everything falls apart. I'm totally taking notes!"

Ava's eyes were sharp as she took a deep breath and read, "Confidence isn't just feeling good when everything's going right. It's believing in yourself, even when you mess up. A mistake doesn't mean you're not good—it's just part of the game. Even the best players make mistakes."

Addie winced, remembering her last strikeout. "So, even if you mess up, you still have to believe you're a good player?"

"Exactly," Ava said, smiling. "And guess what? Confidence is a skill, like hitting or fielding. You don't just have it or not—you can learn it. And it takes practice, just like anything else."

Sophia rested her chin on her hand. "Hmm, easier said than done. Remember Maddy from the Bandits? The girl with the long blond braids? Last game, I struck her out twice—six pitches, and she barely touched the ball! But when she came up again, she wasn't pouting or nervous. She stood tall, like she knew she was still a great hitter. And, well, you know what happened next."

Sophia's eyes widened as she swung an imaginary bat. "Pow!"

Zoe nodded. "She crushed it—a total dinger. She stayed confident after striking out and kept believing in herself. No moping, no pouting, no doubting."

Addie burst out laughing. "No moping, no pouting, no doubting! That's our new team chant. Can you imagine Coach Moore's face?"

Ava giggled and looked back at the book. "Let's see how you stay confident."

Zoe, eyebrows raised, said, "I'm in! What's the first step?"

Ava scanned the page. "**Use positive self-talk.** We've talked about this before. Say things like 'I can do this!' or 'I'll get it next time!' helps you believe in yourself, even when things aren't going your way."

Sophia beamed. "When I'm on deck, I'll think about my game-winning homer last season and tell myself, 'You're a tough hitter. Crush it!'"

"Like we learned before, your self-talk changes how you feel. It can build your confidence or tear it down," Zoe said. "I'm glad we're focusing on what we say to ourselves. What's the next tip?"

"**Use visualization:** Picture yourself succeeding before it happens. It helps your mind believe you can do it, so it feels easier when you actually play." Ava grinned. "We just learned that! It's amazing how all these mental skills work together."

"Yep, I do it every night now. Before bed, I picture myself throwing perfect pitches. I see the batter swing and miss, and I hear the crowd cheer. It really boosts my confidence," Sophia said.

"That's awesome!" Ava said, high-fiving Sophia.

Ava flipped the page, her excitement growing. "You're going to love this. **Create a success diary:** After every game or practice, you write three things you did well—no matter how small. You can use a notebook or your phone."

"Even if it's just hustling or making a solid throw, write it down. Focusing on the good stuff builds your confidence little by little. And it says to read it every day, especially when you're feeling shaky."

"A success diary? That's cool!" Zoe said.

Addie grinned. "So, I think of great plays I've made, like that awesome diving catch last game, and write it down? Even just thinking about it now makes me feel unstoppable!" She jumped to her feet, pumped her fist, then flopped back down.

Sophia nodded. "I'm doing that right after practice today! What about you guys?"

"I'm starting mine, too!" Zoe said, her eyes shining. She could already picture the best moments that would help her shake off mistakes and build her confidence.

Ava's eyes sparkled as she leaned in. "Check out these extra tips."

"**Fan chatter:** If you're nervous about what the fans are saying, imagine they're all talking about how awesome you are. Picture every fan in the stands, saying, 'Wow! She's the best player I've ever seen!' Imagine them cheering every time you swing or make a great catch. That'll boost your confidence fast."

"That's such a cool idea!" Sophia beamed. "I always get nervous when I hear the crowd, but if I imagine they're cheering for me, I'll feel powerful instead of scared."

"Yeah!" Addie grinned. "I love it!"

Ava smiled. "Here's another great tip: **Play against younger players.** Picture yourself playing against kids two years younger and that they're totally afraid of you. Imagine them nervous because they know how good you are. It'll make you feel more confident and less worried about the other team."

Zoe giggled. "That's funny, but it makes sense. I'll feel way more confident knowing I'm the one they're scared of! Big scary me!"

Addie nudged Zoe, pretending to shiver in fear.

The girls burst out laughing.

Ava continued reading. "Here's a good one: **'It's the first day of the season.'** If you've been in a slump, don't keep thinking about it. Pretend today is the first day of the season. It's a fresh start. Everyone's confident on day one, right?"

Sophia nodded. "I love that idea. When I'm not playing well, it sometimes feels like I'll never break out of it. But if I think of it as a fresh start, the slump fades away. Remember what Katie said—each pitch is a new chance, and softball's all about winning the next pitch."

Addie grinned. "Starting fresh is like hitting reset. Forget the bad stuff and just focus on playing your best right now."

"Exactly." Ava nodded. "The journal has one more important tip. **Before every game, expect to play your best.** Check out Katie's note."

Ava held up the book so everyone could see.

Don't just HOPE to play well.

Don't just THINK you'll play well.

EXPECT to play well!

"Before every practice or game, take a minute and think, 'I'm going to play my best today.' Tell yourself, 'Today could be my best day yet,' and believe it! Today is your day!"

Ava read the last line of the chapter aloud. **"Confidence isn't something you just *have*—it's something you *build.*"**

"That's such a great way to end it!" Ava said, smiling. "Addie, can you list all those tips for us?"

"Sure! I've got them right here on my tablet." Addie quickly scrolled through her screen. "Here's the list."

1. Use positive self-talk. Don't beat yourself up after a mistake. Use words that build your confidence instead.

2. Visualize yourself making great plays or smashing base hits.

3. Keep a success diary of things you've done well in practice or in games. It helps remind you that you're a great player, even when things aren't going well. Read it often to build your confidence little by little.

4. If you're nervous about the crowd, imagine every fan is talking about how amazing you are. They can't wait to see your awesome pitches, swings, and plays.

5. Picture yourself playing against a younger team that's afraid of you. They know you're really good, and they're scared to face you.

6. If you are in a slump, pretend today is the first day of the season. None of those bad at-bats happened. It's a fresh start, a reset. Everyone's confident on the first day, right?

7. Expect to play well. Before each game or practice, take a moment to really think about how today can be your best day ever. Don't hope to play well, but **expect** to play well. Make today your day!

"Great job, Tech Girl! Send that to everyone." Ava looked around at the group. "This is really going to help us, especially in big games. Confidence is something we build, so let's start building it!"

"Yeah!" the girls cheered, exchanging fist bumps and high-fives.

Ava turned to the last page slowly. Her eyes widened, and her jaw dropped. "Whoa, Katie left us a final note!"

I hope you liked this book. Be sure to practice and use all the mental game skills you've learned. From now on, your goal in every softball game is to focus on just winning the next pitch. These skills will help you do that. Have fun!

Katie

The girls grinned at each other, their eyes gleaming with determination. They knew the real challenge wasn't just learning the seven mental skills—it was practicing them every single day.

With the Southport City Championship just two weeks away, the pressure was building. But now, armed with the secrets from the journal, they felt more ready than ever. The girls couldn't wait to share what they'd learned with Coach Moore and the team. If the Sting worked hard, sharpened their skills, and stayed mentally tough, they'd be ready for anything.

## Solve These Mystery Questions!

1. What is confidence? Why is it important to believe in yourself when playing softball? Can you remember a time when believing in yourself helped you play better?

2. What tips did Katie share for staying confident? Which one do you like best? How can you use that tip in your next game or practice?

3. Start a success diary. Write down your best hits and plays and remember how they felt. Write three of those here. You can keep it private or share it. Add to it after every practice and game.

4. What will you do before your next game to expect to play well, rather than just hope to play well?

CHAPTER 11

# Southport's City Championship: Time for the Sting to Shine

The sun was shining brightly at Archer Field, with fans in their team gear scrambling to find their seats. All eyes were on the field, where the players stretched and prepared, ready for the action to begin.

This was the day the Southport Sting had been waiting for—the City Championship game. They were facing their toughest rivals, the Carolina Waves. The Waves had won the last three championships, and today, they were hungry for their fourth. Earlier in the season, the Waves crushed the Sting, 7-0, in a tournament. The Waves' star pitcher, Madison Walker, had thrown a one-hitter and struck out every Sting player at least once.

But this time, the Sting was a different team. They had something the Waves didn't — mental game skills they'd learned from a secret journal. They were ready.

As the Sting gathered at the park, Addie walked by the concession stand, hearing the *pop-pop-pop* of popcorn. The salty smell of butter filled the air. She glanced up just in time to dodge a boy carrying a soda and a hotdog dripping with ketchup.

Addie smiled, pulled a piece of gum from her pocket, and popped it into her mouth. She blew a bubble so big it almost covered her face. Giggling, she strolled to the dugout, already picturing her first swing of the day.

Stepping through the gate, Addie paused to enjoy the exciting moment. Coach Moore sat in the dugout, scribbling the lineup on her clipboard. In the outfield, Mia and a few teammates played catch, their laughter drifting on the breeze.

Zoe stood by the backstop, gripping her shiny orange bat, her eyes locked on an imaginary pitch. Hannah, holding her catcher's mask, leaned in as Sophia, the team's star pitcher, whispered last-minute strategies.

"Ready to show the Waves what we've got?" Ava asked, bouncing on her toes.

"Totally," Addie said, her eyes sparkling as she tossed her bat bag into the dugout. "Did you see the trophy? It's taller than me!"

Ava scanned the bleachers. "And check out the crowd! The City Championship has been Southport's biggest game, like, forever."

"And we get to play in it!" Addie's grin widened. "Did you see all those ladies by our dugout wearing matching yellow shirts?"

"Yeah, hard to miss." Ava smiled, tilting her head. "Looks like some kind of class reunion. Their shirts say, 'Southport High, Class of '89.'"

"More fans for us!" Addie pumped her fist. "Go, Sting!"

Zoe bounced into the dugout, bursting with energy. "Are you ready? I am! Let's win this thing!"

"Yep, we're ready. They beat us last time, but we've got our new mental game skills," Addie said, her voice full of confidence.

Ava nodded. "Oh yeah, we've learned so much. Everyone's been practicing, and we look sharp. I can't wait to use our skills today! This is going to be fun!"

Addie tightened her grip on her bat, taking a slow half-swing. "My dad and I went to the cages to practice my pre-pitch routine," she said, her words picking up speed. "I've been filling my success diary, practicing my self-talk, deep breathing, and the 3 Ts. I'm so ready!"

Ava dug through her bat bag and pulled out a sign. "I printed this to remind us of the skills from Katie's journal. I texted Coach Moore, and she's going to hang it by the energy meter."

"That's awesome!" Addie gave Ava a playful slap on the back with her dusty glove.

The crowd buzzed with energy. Shouts of 'Let's go, Sting!', 'You got this!' and 'Expect to play well!' spilled from the bleachers.

*"Expect to play well,"* Addie nodded, repeating the words. "That's been stuck in my head all morning. Like Katie said, 'Don't hope to play well—expect it!'"

"Exactly! Today's our day to shine!" Ava said, already jogging toward the outfield. "Let's get out there and throw."

As Addie jogged toward the outfield, she noticed Sophia, the Sting's pitcher, throwing to Hannah. Sophia's eyebrows were scrunched, and she frowned after each pitch.

"Not again," Sophia muttered, kicking at the dirt. Her go-to pitch, the change-up, wasn't working today. It kept missing the strike zone or didn't change speed like it should.

Sophia bit her lip, staring at the ground as her shoulders slumped in frustration.

Addie slowed her jog, watching as Sophia threw another wild pitch. She stepped closer and called, "You've got this, Sophia! Slow down, breathe, and just focus on the next pitch, not the last one!"

Sophia's eyes brightened as a small smile spread across her face. "You're right. I was getting frustrated, and it just made things worse."

Sophia took a deep breath, scooped up some dirt, and tossed it aside. "Hit your spot. You've got this. You've thrown thousands of strikes," she whispered to herself.

The next pitch zipped straight into Hannah's glove. After a few more fastballs, she tried her change-up. It floated perfectly, landing exactly where she wanted. Sophia's confidence grew with each pitch. Each change-up was smoother than the one before. Every fastball hit its mark. Soon, a big smile spread across her face.

Sophia pointed her glove toward the outfield. "Hey, it worked! Thanks for the reminder, Addie!"

"Anytime," Addie yelled with a grin, before catching a high arcing throw from Ava.

Across the field, the Waves warmed up with quiet confidence. Madison Walker, their star pitcher, fired warm-up pitches to her catcher, each one faster and more precise.

The umpire signaled for both teams to clear the field. It was time to start the game.

As the team gathered in the dugout, Ava could feel the tension rising. She stood in front of her teammates, trying to keep her voice steady despite her nerves. "We've worked hard to get here," she said, looking each player in the eye. "Use your mental game skills and focus on one pitch at a time. Just win the next pitch."

Coach Moore nodded. "Ava's right. The next pitch is the most important one." She pointed to the energy meter. "Keep that meter green! And don't forget Arrows-Out attitudes, no matter what!"

Addie stepped forward, her voice ringing out loud and clear. "Sting on three!"

"One, two, three, STING!" they yelled, their voices echoing into the stands.

Energized and ready, the Sting sprinted onto the field. Chatter filled the air as they took their positions. Sophia's warm-up pitches hit the mark, and the infielders handled grounders like pros. Hannah jogged to the circle, giving Sophia some last-minute advice. Sophia nodded, her ponytail bouncing, as Hannah hustled back behind the plate.

"Play ball!" the umpire yelled, his voice booming over the field, setting the game in motion.

Sophia fired a sharp strike, the ball snapping into Hannah's glove with a satisfying pop. The Sting fans erupted in cheers, their energy fueling team's confidence.

*We've got this. Time to show what we've learned!* Addie thought, smacking her fist into her glove, ready for the next pitch.

For the next few hours, nothing else mattered but the game. Both teams gave it their all—every pitch, every swing, every catch.

The game started with neither team scoring in the first inning. Sophia sent three Waves back to the dugout with two strikeouts and a lazy pop-up. Madison was even sharper. The Waves' ace mowed down Mia, Gracie, and Hannah, not letting any of them touch the ball. With every strikeout, the Sting's spirits dropped a little more.

The Sting trudged back onto the field for the top of the second inning, their shoulders slumped after Madison's domination. Murmurs of "She's too tough" and "We can't hit her" floated through the team. It felt just like last time—getting a hit off Madison seemed impossible.

"Sting! Let's go! Get that energy meter back to green!" a woman's voice bellowed from the stands, cutting through the noise of the crowd.

The Sting heard her and realized low energy wouldn't win this game. It was time to move the energy meter arrow from red to green. They picked up their hustle, their chatter growing louder. Infield practice was sharp, and the team was ready to play their best.

Sophia cruised through the inning, getting the Waves' clean-up hitter to fly out to center field with a perfectly placed fastball. Grounders to Zoe at shortstop and Addie at second easily took care of the next two batters.

"Way to throw strikes, Sophia!" Addie said, slapping her a high-five as they jogged off the field together.

"Thanks. Our awesome defense makes it easy," Sophia said with a nod.

Ava was the first to bat in the bottom of the second inning, with Addie and Zoe to follow. During warm-ups, Madison's fastballs cracked into the catcher's mitt like thunder. After the last warm-up pitch, the catcher yanked off her mitt, shaking her hand from the sting of Madison's heat.

In the on-deck circle, Addie gripped her bat tight, her knuckles turning white. Zoe, adjusting her helmet, stood nearby. Addie glanced over at Zoe, eyes wide. "Wow, she throws hard," she whispered. Memories of facing Madison last time flashed through Addie's mind—she had struck out both times. "I can't hit this girl," Addie muttered. "She's going to strike me out again."

Zoe turned to Addie. "Whoa! Remember your self-talk? You've got to believe you can hit her. You're a good hitter," she said, lifting Addie's spirits.

"Don't say, 'I can't.' Say, 'I can hit this pitcher. I'm an awesome hitter.' Do your routine and take it one pitch at a time. You just have to beat her on one pitch!" Zoe's voice was steady.

Addie took a deep breath, repeating Zoe's words in her mind. She swung a few more times, imagining a pitch right down the middle and her bat sending the ball flying. The knot in her stomach loosened, replaced by excitement. "I can't wait to crush one of her pitches," she whispered, tightening her batting gloves.

The crowd gasped as Ava sent a deep fly ball toward the fence, only for the Waves' speedy center fielder to catch it over her shoulder. The ball shot off the bat like a rocket, farther than anyone on the Sting had hit against Madison all season. A flicker of hope sparked in the dugout.

Addie dropped her warm-up bat and marched to the plate, ready for the challenge ahead. She locked into her pre-pitch routine, determined to focus on just one pitch at a time. As she looked at her focus point on her bat, the crowd's cheers faded. All that mattered was the ball coming out of Madison's hand.

*She looks confident. Addie's doing exactly what we talked about,* Zoe thought, watching her teammate focus.

Addie stood tall in the batter's box, eyes narrowed and jaw clenched. She wasn't scared. She was ready to crush it.

Madison wound up and unleashed a fastball. Addie swung hard, but the ball zipped right past her.

"Strike one!" the umpire shouted.

Addie didn't flinch. She went through her pre-pitch routine: glanced at her coach, took a deep breath, studied her focus point, and locked her eyes on Madison's release point.

With a sly grin, Madison threw a change-up. Addie expected another fastball and was surprised. She swung too early, missing the ball completely.

"Strike two!" the umpire called out.

With two strikes, Addie wasn't her usual nervous self. Instead, she was more focused than ever. *One pitch at a time. Win this next pitch.*

"Look at Addie. She's staying cool," Ava whispered to Hannah. "That's a good sign."

Addie stepped out of the box, went through her routine, then settled back in. Madison fired another fastball, confident she could blow it past her. But Addie was ready. She swung with perfect timing.

*Crack!*

The ball soared deep to right field, and the fielder turned, sprinting after it. The Sting bench gasped. It was the longest ball anyone had ever seen Addie hit. Could it be a homer?

# Southport's City Championship: Time for the Sting to Shine

The ball ricocheted off the top of the fence. Addie bolted past first base. *Faster, run faster!* Addie thought, rounding second and skidding into third in a spray of dirt. Her heart pounded with excitement. She'd done it—she got a hit off Madison, and not just any hit, a triple!

As Addie caught her breath on third, Quinn Jenkins, the Waves' shortstop, jogged over and tapped her leg with her glove. "Nice hit! I thought that one was gone!"

"Thanks!" Addie wheezed, a huge smile spreading across her face. She adjusted her helmet with both hands as her teammates cheered and high-fived in the dugout.

Zoe flashed Addie a thumbs-up as she stepped to the plate, her confidence soaring. With Addie on third, Zoe knew a base hit would give the Sting the lead.

"Hit your pitch, Zoe! Right hitter, right time!" Coach Moore yelled, clapping, trying to be heard over the crowd.

Zoe took a deep breath, focused on the spot on her bat, and locked her eyes on Madison's release point.

With renewed determination, Madison fired her fastest pitch of the day. Zoe swung hard but came up empty.

"Strike one!" the umpire called.

"A little quicker, Zoe! You can get her!" Ava shouted, her voice strong and confident.

*Every pitch is a new chance*, Zoe reminded herself. *Look for the change-up.*

Zoe went through her pre-pitch routine and dug into the batter's box. Madison reached back and fired a blazing fastball. Expecting a change-up, Zoe froze as the fastball sailed right down the middle.

"Steeerike two!" the umpire shouted, punching the air with his right arm.

Panic surged through Zoe. *Two strikes. I'm in trouble. Don't strike out. Whatever you do, don't strike out!* Her heart raced, and her breath quickened as images of striking out flashed in her mind.

Zoe stepped out of the box and looked around. She locked eyes with a woman in the front row, wearing a yellow reunion shirt.

The woman pointed and nodded to Zoe. "Say what you want to happen, not what you're afraid of. You can do it!" she said with a confident smile.

The words sank in instantly. It was the same advice from Katie's journal. "Say what you want to happen, not what you're afraid of," Zoe whispered to herself. She glanced one last time at the mysterious woman. *Could that be Katie?* she wondered.

Zoe shook her head and focused on the task at hand, then took another deep breath and thought, *Hit the ball hard. Hit the ball hard.* The image of striking out faded, replaced by the ball rocketing off her bat.

A wave of calm washed over Zoe as she went through her routine. Her mind quieted, and her eyes locked on Madison's release point. It was just her and the ball, nothing else.

Madison stared at her catcher, shook off a sign, and fired a blazing fastball screaming toward the plate. Zoe swung.

*Bam!*

The bat vibrated in Zoe's hands as the ball shot past a ducking Madison and rocketed into center field. Zoe bolted toward first, her helmet bouncing with each step, and her heart pounding like a drum.

*I did it! I did it!* Zoe thought, rounding first before hustling back to the bag safely.

Addie sprinted home from third, and the Sting took the lead, 1-0.

"Way to go, Zoe!" Sophia's voice rang out above the cheers.

Zoe pumped her fist, a huge smile spreading behind her facemask.

The crowd was roaring, but one voice stood out—the woman in the front row. Zoe couldn't help but look her way again.

"Way to go! I knew you could do it!" the woman shouted, still clapping excitedly.

Madison didn't seem rattled. She took a few deep breaths and fired perfect pitches, striking out Lily and Emma to end the inning.

"Great hit, Addie!" Zoe called as the girls ran back to their positions, still buzzing from the excitement.

"You, too. Way to bring me home," Addie said, scooping up a grounder and tossing it to first. "And hey, thanks for the self-talk reminder. It helped a lot."

Zoe waved Addie over. "Speaking of reminders, did you see that woman in the front row? She's with the reunion group. She reminded me to say what I want to happen, not what I'm afraid of. So instead of 'Don't strike out,' I said, 'Hit the ball hard.' And it worked!"

Addie adjusted her mask. "Whoever she is, that was great advice. Sounds like something Katie would've said."

Zoe paused and slowly watched the mysterious fan in the stands. "That's exactly what I thought…"

## Solve These Mystery Questions!

1. Can you list two or three mental skills the Sting girls used during the game? How did these skills help?

2. What does it mean to "expect to play well" instead of "hope to play well?"

3. Zoe changed her self-talk to focus on what she wanted to happen. How did that help her hit the ball? When can you use positive self-talk like this in your own life?

# CHAPTER 12

# Katie, Is That You?

For the next two tense innings, the score stayed frozen at 1-0 as the Sting clung to their slim lead.

In the top of the fifth inning, Quinn Jenkins, the Waves' shortstop, swung hard. The ball shot past the infield, bouncing safely into left field. The next batter didn't wait long. She hammered Sophia's first pitch, sending the ball zipping into center field, where it skipped just in front of Mia.

Another hit!

Two pitches, two runners on base. The Waves were on fire. Fans jumped to their feet, screaming and clapping as cheers filled the field.

Sophia's eyes went wide. Her heart raced. *What's happening?* she wondered.

Sophia glanced at the Waves' dugout, which had exploded into cheers. Players jumped like they'd already won. Her stomach twisted. Sophia could hear the Waves yelling, "Everyone's getting a hit!" and "It's just like practice!" She felt like everything was closing in on her.

Sweat trickled down Sophia's forehead as she walked to the back of the circle. Her heart raced and her thoughts spun out of control. Sophia shuffled back to the pitching rubber, her breath shallow as she locked eyes with Hannah for the sign. Her next pitch sailed high. Too high! But Hannah jumped and snatched it out of the air, saving it from the backstop.

Sophia couldn't hit the strike zone on the next three pitches. Hannah blocked a change-up in the dirt, followed by two pitches that missed the mark by a mile. Ball four. Bases loaded.

Waves fans erupted, while the Sting side fell silent, holding their breath. Bases loaded. No outs. The Sting clung to their 1-0 lead.

Sophia shook her head. Her pitches were wild. Nothing felt right. "Come on," she muttered under her breath, feeling like she was letting everyone down.

"Throw strikes!" a parent shouted, their voice slicing through the chaos.

"Not helpful!" Sophia huffed, shaking her head as she kicked the dirt.

"Play ball!" the umpire shouted.

Sophia gripped the ball tightly, the seams digging into her palm. *I'll show them*, she thought, winding up and firing her hardest pitch yet. The pitch was fast—really fast—but wild. It sailed over Hannah's glove and slammed into the backstop.

The runner from third dashed for home. Hannah grabbed the rolling ball and tossed it to Sophia, who was charging toward the plate. Bodies tangled together in a big cloud of dust.

"Safe!" the umpire shouted, spreading his arms wide.

The Waves burst from the dugout, celebrating their dust-covered teammate. The runners on second and third clapped wildly. Sophia stood frozen, her mouth hanging open. The score was tied 1-1.

"You've got this, Sophia. We'll get them!" Ava called out, trying to cheer her up.

Sophia paced nervously as the crowd's noise grew louder. One woman's voice rose above the rest, catching Sophia's attention. It was the same woman who had given Zoe advice earlier.

"Take a deep breath and just win this next pitch! One pitch at a time!" she shouted.

*She's right. Just focus on this pitch*, Sophia thought. She walked to the back of the circle, rolling her shoulders and taking deep breaths before glancing at the fan again.

"Just win this pitch! Arrows-Out!" the woman called.

"Win this pitch," Sophia repeated, feeling a wave of calm wash over her.

Alice Hill, the Waves' second baseman, came to the plate, and the umpire shouted, "Play ball!"

Hannah flashed the sign, and Sophia nodded quickly. She imagined the ball flying right over the plate, took a deep breath, wound up, and let it go.

"Steeerike!" the umpire shouted as the batter watched the pitch hit the corner.

"Next pitch," Sophia whispered, rolling the ball in her glove.

The next pitch zipped right on target. Alice swung and missed.

"Steeerike two!" the umpire shouted.

"Get that strikeout, Sophia! You've got this!" Zoe called from shortstop.

Sophia wound up and fired another fastball. Alice didn't move—frozen in place.

"Steeerike three!"

"Great job, Sophia! One down! Get the next one!" Addie shouted, holding one finger up over her head.

Taking it one pitch at a time, Sophia delivered three of her best strikes to the next Waves' batter. The batter didn't have a chance as she swung late each time and struck out. Two outs.

Hannah grinned and tossed the ball back to Sophia, her eyes shining with confidence. "That's how you do it!"

With runners still on second and third, the Sting needed just one more out. The Carolina Waves' cleanup hitter, Marie Garcia, marched to the plate. Towering over the Sting catcher, she stood eye-to-eye with the umpire. Pitchers feared her, and for good reason—Marie had sent plenty of balls over the fence.

Coach Moore squinted, anxiously rubbing her chin before motioning for the outfielders to step back.

Marie tugged on her batting gloves and shot Sophia a fierce glare. As she warmed up, Hannah could feel the breeze from each of Marie's powerful swings. Jaw clenched, Marie dug her back foot into the dirt, daring Sophia to throw a strike.

Sophia nodded at the sign and wound up. She unleashed her fastest pitch yet, and Marie was ready.

*Crack!*

A line drive rocketed down the third-base line, looking like a sure hit. Without hesitation, Ava dove to her left, snatching it out of mid-air. She hit the ground hard, but the ball stayed firm in her glove.

"Out!" the umpire shouted.

The Sting bench and fans erupted in wild cheers. They got out of a big jam! The score remained tied 1-1.

Marie slammed her bat down, her mouth wide open in disbelief.

"Great play!" Sophia said as she and the team sprinted off the field.

"Way to pitch out of trouble!" Ava said.

Sophia sat down between Addie and Zoe on the bench, pointing toward the stands. "Who's the lady in the reunion shirt sitting in the front row?"

"Don't know. Why?" Addie asked, looking confused.

"She reminded me to take my breaths and just focus on winning the next pitch. It helped."

Zoe jumped in, "That's the same lady who told me to say what I want to happen, not what I'm afraid of. I heard her say 'Arrows-Out' earlier, too. Reminds me of something Katie would say. You don't suppose…?"

Addie paused, glancing at the fan again. *Who is she?* She wondered, rubbing her chin. "I don't know. Maybe…"

The game went on as Madison quickly retired the Sting batters in order in the bottom of the fifth.

"Last inning, let's hold'em here!" Addie called out.

The Sting players sprinted to their positions for the top of the sixth. Their energy meter was in the green.

Sophia, with newfound confidence, struck out the Waves' first batter. The next batter hit a grounder toward Addie. She tried to stop it, but the ball skipped off her glove. Scrambling, she threw to first—but too late.

"Safe!" the umpire shouted, waving his arms.

Now it was the Carolina fans' turn to cheer. The go-ahead run was on base.

"Great, just great!" Addie grumbled, feeling tension build up inside her. *Okay, reset. Time to reset!* she thought.

Addie took a deep breath, scooped up some dirt, and tossed it aside. "Gone!" she whispered, smacking her glove. "You're a great fielder. Time to make a great play!"

The Waves' shortstop, Quinn Jenkins, stepped up to the plate. A solid hitter, she had already singled earlier in the game.

*Just make this next pitch,* Sophia thought, her confidence unshaken. She fired a fastball low and on the outside corner.

Quinn swung with everything she had.

*Wham!* The ball exploded off her bat—a line drive straight at Addie, who snagged it. The Waves' runner, halfway to second, froze. Addie fired the ball to Emma. Double play! Three outs!

The Sting players cheered and their fans roared so loud it felt like the ground was shaking. Across the way, the once-loud Waves' fans and players fell silent.

Zoe gave Addie a pat on the back as they walked to the dugout.

"Great reset, second baseman! Nice job using the 3 Ts!" the lady in the front row called out, smiling.

Addie looked up in surprise. "Thanks!"

Zoe stopped in her tracks, her jaw dropping. "The 3 Ts? That's the same lady who gave me and Sophia advice! You don't think it's…" she whispered.

"I wondered the same thing before, but what are the chances? I mean…" Addie said. "That's impossible, isn't it?"

* * *

The game shifted to the bottom of the sixth, with the score still locked at 1-1.

Coach Moore called the team together. "Okay, girls. One run wins this thing! We've got Ava, Addie, and Zoe up. Addie, if Ava gets on, you're bunting."

Addie nodded. "You got it, Coach."

Madison finished her warm-up pitches, her fastball still snapping into the catcher's mitt. The umpire signaled to play ball.

The stands buzzed with energy as fans yelled for their team.

Ava did her routine and stepped into the batter's box. Standing tall, with her eyes narrowed in focus, she was ready for the challenge.

Madison's first pitch was a fastball down the middle. Ava swung and hit a low line drive that skipped in front of the center fielder. The fielder bobbled it for a second. Ava thought about going to second but wisely stopped and scrambled back to first. The Sting had the winning run on base.

A hush fell over the crowd as Addie stepped up to the plate. She knew she'd be bunting, and so did everyone in the park.

"First and third, move up! She's bunting!" the Carolina coach shouted, waving his arms.

Addie's heart pounded. *I have to get this bunt down,* she thought. *But they're right on top of me!* She took a deep breath to calm down.

Madison's first pitch was a high fastball. Addie jabbed her bat out, but the ball skipped off the top, flying back to the backstop. Strike one.

*Wow! She's still throwing fast,* Addie thought, her eyes widening as she stepped out of the box.

"See yourself catching the ball with your bat. Imagine the perfect bunt. Picture it!" called the now familiar voice from the stands.

Zoe, standing on deck, stared toward the stands. *It's her again*, she thought.

The words stuck with Addie. She closed her eyes, picturing the perfect bunt. Remembering Katie's journal, she smiled. *They can't stop me. Best bunter in the world*, Addie thought.

Madison's next pitch came right down the middle. Addie squared. *Thud!* The bunt dropped perfectly in front of the plate. Ava sprinted to second base. The Waves' third baseman scooped up the ball and threw it to first.

"Out!" shouted the first base umpire on a close play.

It was so close that Sting fans started grumbling loudly from the bleachers.

Addie jogged back to the dugout, her teammates rushing to congratulate her on the perfect bunt.

Addie sat down next to Sophia. "I heard someone remind me to visualize the bunt. I did, and it worked great!" she said, still catching her breath.

"Was it Coach Moore?" Sophia asked.

"No, it was that same lady in the front row! It really worked!" Addie said, pushing strands of wet hair from her face as she took off her helmet.

Fans leaned forward on the edge of their seats as Zoe stepped up to the plate. A base hit would win the game. Her heart pounded, and her mind raced. She glanced out at Ava on second. Ava motioned for her to breathe and go through her pre-pitch routine.

Zoe did just that. Like a sharp flashlight, her eyes locked on Madison's release point. The nerves were gone; her mind was clear. It was just her and the ball.

Madison's first pitch came right down the middle, and Zoe swung, ripping a foul straight back for strike one. She drilled another foul ball on the next pitch. With the count at 0-2, Zoe locked in on the release point each time and fouled off two more pitches.

With each foul ball, Madison's frustration grew. The Waves' ace wanted the strikeout, but Zoe kept hitting her best fastballs. Madison fired another pitch. The fastball zipped straight toward the plate.

Zoe swung with all her strength, feeling the bat vibrate up her arms.

The crowd held its breath for a moment before erupting in cheers. "Go, go, go!"

Zoe sprinted toward first, her eyes tracking the ball as it dropped into the gap between the center fielder and right fielder, rolling to the fence.

Coach Moore waved frantically, sending Ava home to score the winning run. The Sting had done it! City Champions!

The Sting players stormed out of the dugout, cheering wildly as they surrounded Ava at home plate, their voices echoing across the field. Then they mobbed Zoe, shouting, hugging, and playfully tapping her helmet in celebration.

The Sting fans roared.

"You did it!" Ava shouted to Zoe. "That hit was so clutch!"

*I did it. No... we did it,* Zoe thought, her heart still pounding from the excitement. The mental game skills from Katie's journal made the difference.

As the cheers faded and they shook hands with the Waves, the girls gathered around the trophy, grinning as their parents snapped pictures. Coach Moore chatted with a reporter from the *Southport News*.

But while the others laughed and chatted, Addie lingered on the field, her eyes drawn toward the stands. She noticed the high school reunion group near the Sting dugout.

"Hey, look! It's the woman who kept giving us advice. Let's go thank her," Addie said, nudging Zoe.

"Great idea! She was saying the exact same things as in Katie's journal," Zoe said, her eyes wide with excitement. "She told me to focus on what I want to happen, not what I'm afraid of."

"She told me to just focus on winning the next pitch and to play Arrows-Out," Sophia said, nodding.

"Whoa! She reminded me to visualize before my bunt. And you won't believe this. Earlier, she even complimented me on using the 3 Ts!" Addie exclaimed.

"No way!" Ava gasped. "The 3 Ts? How does she know all that? You don't think… it's Katie, do you?"

"Maybe," Addie murmured, eyes locked on the woman. "Let's go thank her—maybe we'll find out who she really is."

The girls were just steps away from the mysterious fan when another woman came up and gave her a friendly hug. "Diamond Girl! It's you! How've you been?"

Ava and the girls froze in their tracks, their eyes widening in disbelief.

"Diamond Girl? Did she just really say that?" Addie whispered, her heart skipping a beat.

The others, too stunned to speak, nodded.

They stood watching the reunion until the woman turned to them with a wide, friendly smile. "Great game, girls! Congrats on winning the championship!"

"Thank you!" they said together.

"Hi, I'm Ava, and here's Zoe, Addie, and Sophia. We just wanted to thank you for the advice—it really helped us!"

"You're welcome. You all played with great energy, and I noticed your pre-pitch routines," the woman said with a smile.

"Ask her! Ask her!" Addie whispered, giving Ava a nudge.

Ava took a deep breath. "Is your name... Katie Parker?" she asked, as all eyes focused on the woman.

The woman shook her head. "No, it's not," she replied with a soft smile.

The girls' hearts sank, their heads drooping in disappointment. They had been so sure they'd solved the mystery of Katie and the old softball journal.

Then the woman looked at them, her smile widening. "But it used to be. I'm Katie Burns now. I'm in town for my class reunion, but I used to live in Southport. I played softball here for years."

Addie's excitement burst out before she could stop herself. "And you won the City Championship in 1983!" she blurted.

Looking confused, Katie said, "Yes, we did… but how do you know that? How'd you guess my name?"

Ava quickly explained how they'd found the softball box at the yard sale and how the mental game skills from Katie's journal helped them this season.

Katie's eyes lit up. "That's amazing! I lost track of that box when we moved years ago."

"We still have it! And we'd love to give it back to you," Ava said. "Maybe… you could finally write that book you always dreamed of," she added with a hopeful grin.

"That's a fantastic idea! How about you girls help me write it? We could even share the story of how you found the journal and how it helped you win the City Championship."

"Deal!" the girls shouted together.

\* \* \*

In the following months, Katie and the girls poured their hearts into writing a book to help young softball players master the mental game. It focused on seven key mental skills that help players do the most important thing—*win the next pitch*. The Sting players shared stories from their unforgettable season, making the book even more special.

Today, that very book sits proudly in the Southport Public Library. Its lessons continue to inspire thousands of young softball players across the country. And the title? *Softball Secrets! Solving the Mysteries of the Mental Game.*

## Solve These Mystery Questions!

1. What reminders did the mystery fan give the girls? Which one do you think helped them the most?

2. Did you guess Katie was at the game? How did you feel when the girls got to meet her?

3. Katie taught the girls that the main goal is to be 100% ready for the next pitch. She shared seven skills to help them. Which skills helped you the most now that you've finished the book?

## COACHES' GUIDE

# Softball Secrets! Solving the Mysteries of the Mental Game

Coaches!

Thank you for guiding your players through *Softball Secrets! Solving the Mysteries of the Mental Game.* This book helps young athletes (ages 10-14) develop their physical skills while mastering the mental aspects of the game. As a coach, you play a crucial role in teaching these mental strategies. This guide offers practical tools to help your team succeed.

In this guide, you'll find summaries for each chapter, fun practice activities, and questions to discuss with your team. These resources will help you show your players how to use mental skills to build confidence and prepare for any challenge on the field.

Let's get started and unlock the secrets that will help your players take their game to the next level!

**Main Lessons and Goals of *Softball Secrets!***

This book focuses on key mental skills that every young athlete should learn and use in their practices and games. The key lessons and goals include:

## 1. Focusing on Just Winning the Next Pitch

- Players will learn that each pitch is an opportunity to make a difference. This helps them focus on what they can control at that moment instead of worrying about the whole game.

## 2. Building High Energy and a Positive Attitude

- Players will understand the importance of showing up with energy and a good attitude every pitch. They'll learn how this can inspire the whole team and lead to better performance.

## 3. Controlling Emotions

- Players will practice ways to stay calm and focused, even when things get tough. This helps them keep their minds clear so they can perform their best under pressure.

## 4. Bouncing Back Quickly After Mistakes

- This lesson teaches players how to bounce back quickly after an error. With a simple reset routine, the 3 Ts, players can clear their minds and get ready for the next play.

## 5. Creating Smart Pre-Pitch Routines

- The book helps players build effective routines before each pitch. These routines keep them focused and ready, without relying on superstitions.

## 6. Using Visualization to Boost Performance

- Players will learn how to picture themselves succeeding before it happens. Visualization helps them feel ready for big moments and play with confidence.

### 7. The Power of Positive Self-Talk

- Players will practice using encouraging and positive words with themselves. They'll learn that their own thoughts can make a big difference in how they play and how confident they feel.

### 8. Blocking Out Distractions and Regaining Focus

- This lesson teaches players how to ignore distractions, like the crowd or their own worries, and focus only on what they need to do next.

### 9. Staying Confident When Things Aren't Going Well

- Players will find out how to stay confident, even if they make mistakes or the game isn't going their way. They will learn how to remind themselves of their strengths and stay positive.

By teaching your players these lessons, you'll help them build mental strength, focus, and confidence—skills that will not only improve their game but also help them grow as people.

It's recommended that you assign a chapter or two at a time, then discuss what your players have learned. Introduce team activities and practice drills to reinforce their learning.

### Chapter 1- A Box of Softball Secrets

The girls, led by Ava, stumble upon a mysterious yard sale where they find a box filled with old softball memorabilia. Among the items is a journal with the title *Softball Secrets*, sparking their curiosity about its former owner, Katie Parker. The girls decide to investigate and uncover the secrets inside, hoping to improve their game.

Team Activities - Chapter 1

1. Assign the chapter and ask your players to write responses to the review questions.

2. Ask your team what they think "the mental game" means and why it's important. See what they already know about any of the mental game skills.

## Chapter 2 – Just Win the Next Pitch!

Back in Ava's treehouse, the girls crack a code inside the journal and discover the mantra, "Win the next pitch." They learn the importance of focusing on one pitch at a time and how mastering this mental skill can change the game. This marks the beginning of their journey to learning the mental game.

Team Activities - Chapter 2

1. Assign the chapter and ask your players to write responses to the review questions.

2. Ask, "What's the main goal of every player in every game?" (Hint: It's about focusing on just winning the next pitch.)

3. Design "Win the Next Pitch" reminders, such as laminated posters for the dugout or bag tags, to reinforce the message. (Luggage tags from the dollar store are great to use.)

4. As a team, explore the seven skills that give players the best chance of winning the next pitch. Ask, "Which of these mental game skills do you need to work on and why?" Get everyone's ideas and examples.

## Chapter 3 – Be a Leader: Control Your Energy and Attitude

The journal introduces the concept of the importance of one's energy and attitude, explaining the difference between an Arrows-Out and Arrows-In mindset. The girls understand that it's their responsibility to themselves and their team to approach every pitch with high energy and a positive attitude.

Team Activities - Chapter 3

1. Assign the chapter and ask your players to write responses to the review questions.

2. Ask, "What are things you can and cannot control during a game?" Point out that playing with high energy and a good attitude are completely under their control.

3. Encourage your players to commit to playing with high energy and a positive attitude, regardless of what has happened during the game.

4. Ask each player to share examples of what Arrows-In and Arrows-Out players look like during a game.

5. Create a cool energy meter for your team and post it in the dugout.

## Chapter 4 – Reset and Win

Through deep breathing and the 3 Ts—**t**ake a breath, **t**hrow away the mistake, **t**ell yourself something positive—the girls learn how to handle pressure during intense game situations. This chapter highlights the importance of resetting after mistakes.

Team Activities - Chapter 4

1. Assign the chapter and ask your players to write responses to the review questions.

2. Ask how players feel after making a mistake and what usually happens if they can't shake it off.

3. Talk about why having a "reset button" can help players forget mistakes and focus on the next pitch.

4. Practice deep breathing as a team. Make sure everyone is doing it correctly.

5. Discuss the 3 Ts of resetting and have players show how they would use these strategies in a game. Coaches, remind your players to use the 3 Ts when they make a mistake in practice. Players need these steps to become automatic during games.

6. Coaches, be sure to positively reinforce the 3 Ts reset when you notice players applying it in practice and games.

## Chapter 5 – These Bulldogs Bite!

The Sting face a tough game against the undefeated Bulldogs. They get a chance to try out some of the mental game skills they've learned so far.

Addie struggles with self-doubt after striking out but later learns to reset using mental skills from the journal, which helps her make a game-saving play.

Team Activities - Chapter 5

1. Assign the chapter and ask your players to write responses to the review questions.

2. Gather feedback from your players about their progress and how they've applied what they've learned so far. This is a great time to review and practice deep breathing, the 3 Ts, and reinforce playing with high energy and an Arrows-Out attitude.

## Chapter 6 – Focus Your Flashlight: Blocking Out Distractions

The girls explore how to block out distractions, using their "focus flashlight" technique to keep their minds locked on the next pitch. They practice staying in control during chaotic game environments, understanding the power of focus.

Team Activities - Chapter 6

1. Assign the chapter and ask your players to write responses to the review questions.

2. Ask, "What does it feel like to be fully focused during a game?"

3. Discuss the flashlight analogy and how they have the power to aim the beam where they want during a game. Ask, "Where should your flashlight be aimed when batting, fielding, or pitching?"

4. Talk about what things can distract them during a game and ask the team what three steps they can take to quickly get focused again if distracted.

5. Get everyone to share their special phrase or phrases that help them refocus. Encourage them to write their phrase(s) down and keep it in their bat bag. Teach them to use the refocus phase during practice.

## Chapter 7 – Talk Like a Champ: Make Your Mind Your MVP

The girls dive into the power of self-talk, learning how to shut down negative thoughts and replace them with positive, empowering ones. This chapter highlights how mental self-talk can either weaken or strengthen confidence.

Team Activities - Chapter 7

1. Assign the chapter and ask your players to write responses to the review questions.

2. Ask, "What is self-talk, and why do you think it's important?"

3. Ask for examples of negative and positive self-talk they've used or heard before.

4. Talk about how positive self-talk isn't just for sports. Where else could it help?

5. Review the self-talk tips and talk about how your team can use them during their next game.

6. Have players pair up, with one player making a negative self-talk statement and the other player changing it to positive self-talk. Switch roles.

## Chapter 8 – Pre-Pitch Routines: Stop Thinking So You Can Start Hitting

Ava teaches the team the four-step pre-pitch routine to turn off their thoughts and focus entirely on the pitch. This proven skill helps the girls react faster and hit better, improving their performance. The Sting are amazed at the results.

Team Activities - Chapter 8

1. Assign the chapter and ask your players to write responses to the review questions.

2. Discuss why pre-pitch routines are helpful and why the pre-pitch routine Ava teaches is better than their superstitious pre-pitch routine.

3. Have players imagine they're walking to home plate. What are the four steps of their routine?

4. Talk to each player about their focus point. Make sure it's something on the bat that's small and unique. They study the fine details like they've never seen it. The goal is to prime the brain for external (outside their own mind) narrow (laser-like) focus. The eyes go immediately to the release point (external narrow target). Thinking will stop and they will be in the best position to just react to the pitch. The better a player gets at doing this, the better hitter they will become.

5. Practice pre-pitch routines in the batting cage using front toss or a pitching machine. Make sure they take their time to get it right. Too often, players want to hurry through it, especially the focus point. You want your players to look at the focus point until there are zero thoughts, even if it takes a few extra seconds. The goal during initial training is to make sure they experience what it's like to hit without thinking. Don't rush the routine when they're first learning. The pre-pitch routine gets quicker with practice.

6. In batting practice and before games, have players do their routine like it's a real game. Rehearsing this, even a few times, pays off later. Again, this type of practice can be done with simple front toss, no live pitching needed.

## Chapter 9 – The Secret Skill: Seeing It Before You Do It

Visualization is introduced as a key mental tool to prepare for success. The girls practice mentally rehearsing game situations, imagining their actions vividly to build confidence and prepare for high-pressure moments.

Team Activities - Chapter 9

1. Assign the chapter and ask your players to write responses to the review questions.

2. Incorporate visualization during practice sessions by having players relax on the floor, close their eyes, while you guide them through different game scenarios. There are YouTube videos that can help your team master these skills.

3. Give your team a homework assignment to practice visualization for at least 5-10 minutes before bed. Be sure to follow up to make sure they do this and get their feedback.

4. Because bunting is such an important skill in softball, go over the pre-pitch routine when bunting, which includes getting the sign, taking a deep breath, using positive self-talk, visualizing the perfect bunt, and feeling the satisfaction of knowing the other team can't stop you.

**Chapter 10 – No More Doubt: How to Play with Confidence**

The final chapter in the journal focuses on confidence as a skill to be practiced and built. The girls learn to use positive self-talk, visualization, and a success diary to strengthen their belief in themselves, even after mistakes.

Team Activities - Chapter 10

1. Assign the chapter and ask your players to write responses to the review questions.

2. Reinforce the idea that all players, at every level, struggle with confidence sometimes.

3. Have players share what it feels like when they've lost confidence. What does it feel like when you are really confident?

4. Give each player a small notebook and have them create their own success diary. Tell them that this diary can be kept private.

5. Ask which of the confidence-building ideas they like best and encourage them to try these during practice and games.

## Chapter 11 – Southport's City Championship: Time for the Sting to Shine

In the championship game against the Carolina Waves, the Sting use all the mental skills they've learned to stay calm under pressure, focusing on winning each pitch. Will these skills be enough to win the City Championship?

## Chapter 12 – Katie, Is That You?

In a tense showdown, the Southport Sting fight to maintain their slim lead against the Carolina Waves. Sophia, struggling under pressure, regains her focus with the help of a mysterious fan in the stands, allowing her to pitch out of a bases-loaded jam. The Sting's defense shines, and Zoe delivers the game-winning hit in the final inning. After the victory, the girls approach the fan, suspecting she might be the legendary Katie from the journal. She reveals she is indeed Katie, and together, they plan to write a book to share the mental game secrets that helped them win.

Team Activities - Chapter 11 & 12

1. Have players list the seven mental game skills the Sting learned. Ask them which skills they found most helpful.

2. Talk about how the Sting used their new mental skills in the City Championship.

3. Make a poster of the overall goal of winning the next pitch and the seven skills that help you do that. Hang it in the dugout.

4. Ask the players to share their knowledge with their parents, as parents are great at reinforcing these skills. Also, encourage the team to reinforce each other.

5. Talk to every player one on one about their mental game skills. See which skills they're confident in using and which ones might need extra practice.

\* \* \*

Final Tips for Coaches

1. Pay attention to your behavior and body language. When adversity hits during a game (and it will), all your players' eyes will be on you. You want your players to stay calm and confident, so make sure to model that! A coach sent me this useful tip. He had his wife video him while coaching so he could review his actions and body language.

2. For hitters, we don't want them thinking anything at the time of the pitch, just reacting. This is why the specific pre-pitch routine in this book is so crucial. As a coach, make sure that you are not "over-coaching" while your hitter is getting in the box or is in the box. Your instructions, while well-meaning, will probably add to mental clutter, and that isn't what we want.

3. Have your players KEEP this book. They can reread it before each season and will pick up things they didn't learn the first time.

4. Finally, keep working on these mental game skills all season. They're just as important as physical skills. Consistent practice is the key to success!

## Concentration Grid

| 04 | 15 | 11 | 24 | 08 |
|----|----|----|----|----|
| 25 | 03 | 19 | 02 | 12 |
| 05 | 16 | 09 | 17 | 20 |
| 14 | 07 | 21 | 06 | 22 |
| 01 | 13 | 10 | 23 | 18 |

## Concentration Grid

| 07 | 12 | 21 | 25 | 05 |
|----|----|----|----|----|
| 20 | 03 | 14 | 06 | 10 |
| 04 | 18 | 02 | 17 | 22 |
| 11 | 09 | 23 | 08 | 24 |
| 01 | 16 | 19 | 13 | 15 |

## Concentration Grid

| 05 | 14 | 01 | 22 | 09 |
|----|----|----|----|----|
| 04 | 17 | 10 | 02 | 18 |
| 08 | 11 | 16 | 07 | 21 |
| 13 | 06 | 25 | 12 | 19 |
| 03 | 15 | 24 | 20 | 23 |

# Acknowledgments

As this book finds its way into the world, I want to take a moment to thank the people who helped make it possible. Writing a book is never done alone—it takes a team of wonderful people working together to create something special.

First, a big thank you to Cynthia Hilston and Olivia Fisher. Your sharp eyes and thoughtful editing made the words in this book clearer and stronger. You've helped me become a better writer, and I'm so grateful for all your hard work on this project.

To my wife, Dianne, thank you for always being there for me. Your patience, support, and smart ideas have meant the world to me. You've helped shape this book in so many ways, from reading my drafts to sharing great thoughts on the story. I couldn't have done this without you.

Finally, thank you to all my readers. As a self-published author, your willingness to share my books with others has meant so much to me. I am deeply thankful for each one of you. Knowing that you're excited about my books makes me want to keep writing more stories.

With all my thanks,
Curt

# About the Author

Dr. Curt Ickes, a licensed clinical psychologist and sport psychology expert, has dedicated his career to combining psychological principles with athletic performance, particularly in baseball. With over 30 years of teaching experience, he now holds the title of Emeritus Faculty at Ashland University, where he continues to support the success of the AU baseball team. Besides his work with the Eagles, he collaborates with various baseball and softball teams and has served as the sport psychologist for the professional baseball team, the Lake Erie Crushers.

Dr. Ickes is the bestselling author of *Win the Next Pitch!*, *Pitch by Pitch!*, and *You Got This!*, all of which introduce young baseball and softball players to key mental game strategies. His first book, *Mental Toughness: Getting the Edge*, is geared toward high school and college athletes looking to master more advanced mental game skills. All of his books are available on Amazon.com.

Dr. Ickes' works not only help young athletes excel on the field but also instill valuable life lessons. His mental game strategies build confidence, foster teamwork, and equip players with the emotional resilience to navigate both the highs and lows of sports—and life.

Made in the USA
Middletown, DE
16 November 2024

64408044R10091